OUT
of
GRIEF

Singing

A MEMOIR OF
MOTHERHOOD
AND LOSS

CHARLENE DIEHL

Signature

EDITIONS

Cover design by Relish Design.
Photo of Charlene Diehl by Jenny Bisch.

This book was printed on Ancient Forest Friendly paper.
Printed and bound in Canada by Marquis Book Printing Inc.

We acknowledge the support of the Canada Council for the Arts and the Manitoba Arts Council for our publishing program.

Library and Archives Canada Cataloguing in Publication

Diehl, Charlene, 1961-
    Out of grief, singing / Charlene Diehl.

ISBN 978-1-897109-44-1

    1. Newborn infants--Death. 2. Parental grief.
3. Bereavement.

I. Title.

BF575.G7D54 2010   155.9'37   C2010-902363-3

Signature Editions
P.O. Box 206, RPO Corydon, Winnipeg, Manitoba, R3M 3S7
www.signature-editions.com

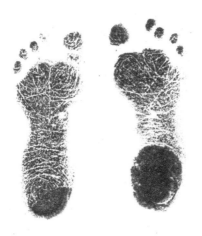

Chloe Denise
November 22–28, 1995

WHEN THE BOUGH BREAKS

November – December 1995

These are the scars
that empty us
into our lives.

— Robert Kroetsch

Tuesday, November 21, afternoon

I'M PERCHED ON THE TABLE in my obstetrician's examining room, waiting for him to come in. Traces of the November drizzle still lodge in my hair, and the paper sheet crackles as I search for a comfortable position.

I'm here for a routine twenty-eight-week check-up. My regular appointment has been delayed by a few days, but I'm into my third trimester so waiting a few days hasn't worried me. I haven't been worried about anything, actually. It's not that I'm naïve, but I have the special innocence of an expectant mother. I'm in the thrall of pregnancy, swept along on a trajectory that won't be hurried and won't be slowed. I'm simply filled up with wonder.

Because I'm in my thirties, I'm in the category of "older mothers," but I don't feel older—I'm in great physical health, and pregnancy suits me. I feel robust and powerful, as if I've been placed at the very centre of the turning world. It piques me to think of myself as older, but I understand too. My husband Bill and I spent our twenties living on scholarships and teaching assistantships—we had set our sights on academic goals rather than jobs and families. With fresh PhDs in hand, mine in literature, his in cell biology, we're just now heading into these larger life narratives. We have moved ourselves to the rolling green landscapes of southern Ontario. I've settled into an academic position teaching Canadian literature at a college on the University of Waterloo campus. I thrive on the challenge, and am inspired by the students. Bill followed me here, and has taken over a dynamic research program at a university laboratory. Against the odds, we're an academic couple who have survived graduate school and found work that satisfies us both. Now is our time: we have a home we love, a sprawling network of friends and family, and the promise of a new baby.

I check my watch again, and my eyes flick toward the door — it remains resolutely closed. I've been relaxed about this pregnancy, but at the moment, I'm starting to feel insecure: I've just offered my arm three times for the standard blood pressure tests, and my readings have been high each time. Bill stands off to the side of the room and I, in my ripe-plum bewilderment, prop myself on the table.

I actually met this doctor for the first time less than a year ago, a bitter January day. He was the doctor on call when I was admitted to the emergency ward, suddenly bleeding twelve weeks into my first pregnancy. I was doing my best to convince myself that I was experiencing one of those normal challenges of early pregnancy, but I knew it was wishful thinking: the bleeding was heavy. We hadn't spoken openly about this pregnancy to our friends, but my body had been invested, and my heart too. I was sick, there in that hive of medical demands, and I was dismayed. Dr Halmo stepped into my anguish. He was gentle and direct, and he laid his hand on me as he spoke to us of this hard thing. I felt him there like an anchor.

Of course, many women miscarry — in the early weeks and months of this year, several of my friends have surprised me with their own experiences with this private misery. About a million miracles go into creating a new human, and when one or two of them don't quite come together according to plan, the maternal body responds. Mine had. Follow-up tests showed no reason for ongoing concern; we should certainly try again.

I admit that trepidation trailed me like a shadow during the first weeks of this pregnancy too, warning against expectation. But when I sailed past the twelve-week mark without incident, I left the fear zone and felt buoyant, expansive — a literalized metaphor. Pregnancy is an adventure, a hijacking of sorts, and though innumerable books litter the floor at my side of the bed, I know I can't read and think my way to where this is taking me. I am along for the ride, a willing passenger.

As I rearrange myself on the examining table, I take stock of my inner weather. I've had no bleeding, no swelling, no headaches. I've noticed that I'm a bit breathless after my half-hour walk to the university, but I don't have as much lung capacity as the baby grows. I'm also more short-tempered than usual — I put that down to a collision of academic responsibilities and the demands of pregnancy. High blood pressure? I take another look at my ankles, no sign of swelling. I listen to Bill's nervous pacing.

A few minutes later, the doctor enters and greets us both. He's more serious than usual, intent. He lays his hands on my round belly, feels the baby. Then he measures to the top of my uterus, measures again, makes notes in my chart. He is quiet for a moment, then shakes his head with concern. *You have significant protein in your urine,* he says, *and these blood pressure readings are high.* He checks for swelling along my shinbone, asks if my head aches. I actually feel fine, but worry is ricocheting around this room now. Something is not right.

Shall we keep track of pressure readings and call you with updates? I say. It's a strange sensation: I hear my own voice, measured and practical, even as I feel a crack opening up under my feet. It's a yawning dark place, a nightmare place, a place I will not imagine.

The doctor instructs Bill to take me directly to the hospital. I want to go home and at least pack some clothes and books, gather my things. No, says the doctor, there isn't time.

My mind reels. I walked into this office from a normal day — a day of toast crumbs and classes, a day of low cloud and unread email and a boisterous lunch with colleagues, a day in the seventh month of inventing a new life. I will walk back out of here, into a different life. How is this possible?

I have crossed a threshold I couldn't see. I have become an emergency.

Tuesday, November 21, evening

BARELY THREE HOURS LATER, I AM CAPTIVE to a body with its own agenda. Several times, I have been whisked in a wheelchair down the shining corridors of Grand River Hospital on the off chance I can be squeezed into the ultrasound technician's overbooked schedule. The blood pressure readings continue to climb; it looks like I'll be transferred to a bigger hospital an hour away, one equipped to handle fragile babies. I'm in a vortex, a whispered frenzy.

Bill has fled to pack pyjamas and a book or two. He will surprise us both by remembering my slippers, a toothbrush, and the address book. Inspired, he will slip in a photo of my family and a floppy-eared bunny that we've given each other every Easter for years. He will forget to pack anything for himself.

By suppertime, I'm on a gurney at the hospital elevator. When the doors open, the ambulance driver takes in my shape, asks if I'm in labour. I shake my head, but I'm falling away from language now. A nurse enters with demands for speed. *Lights and siren?* wonders the driver. *Absolutely*, she says, and waves us out.

In the back of that ambulance, I lose my bearings. I sway erratically around curves and corners, rattle along the stretches of highway. Occasionally, dimly, I hear a siren somewhere in the larger world, imagine us passing through major intersections, cars pausing briefly as we pass. I hear the hushed conversation — aimless, familiar — of the attending nurses, but I can't see them: my eyes are closed against a sudden crushing headache and the assault of the rock-and-roll the driver has chosen as the soundtrack for this fast drive.

I beg for quiet. I get sympathetic murmurs from the nurses, but perhaps they can't hear me, or perhaps I've forgotten how to speak. I seem to be a long way from my own moving mouth; I am descending into interior caverns of pain and worry, listening for subsonic messages from my body, from my baby. The world, pounding in at my ears and eyes, is an affliction, an intrusion. I fly inside, fold myself around the precious one floating in the dark of my belly.

When the ambulance finally arrives at Chedoke-McMaster, it's dark. I come to a stop in a room with a bed, a reclining chair, and a lamp with hardly enough light to read by. Immediately, I am strapped to the wheezing bulk of a machine which will track my climbing blood pressure and beep inscrutable messages to the doctors and nurses who patrol this world.

I huddle in that bed, fearful and stubborn, skewered by an illness I know almost nothing about. Until Bill arrives from his harried drive along unfamiliar highways, I am alone in a dizzying whirl of people. At one point, a specialist brings a circle of students to look at the images on the mobile ultrasound machine. The strangers all gaze at a shadowscape, exchange significant glances, communicate in medical shorthand. I am stung by the specialist's brisk cheer, and I feel excluded from the ring of initiates looking at the mysterious shapes on the ultrasound monitor. I feel disoriented and insecure, hurled into a nightmare game nobody will explain.

I am weary and intimidated and very ill. The abyss is opening beneath me: demon voices whisper, *your baby might die.*

What the monitor cannot show are the tendrils of love which curl around a floating miracle, the slow reach of a mother-self, instinctive, interior, wordless. I follow those tendrils and find my way toward sleep. When I swim awake in the night, I feel Bill's solid warmth in the room, see him reading in the low light.

PRE-ECLAMPSIA, SOMETIMES KNOWN AS TOXEMIA, is a serious disease of pregnancy. It is characterized by high blood pressure — pregnancy-induced hypertension — and protein in the mother's urine. The clamp in the word has just the right ring to it: for reasons that are still not clear, the chemistry of the pregnant body causes the mother's arteries to kink up like poorly stored garden hoses, challenging her circulatory system and liver and kidney function. It can lead to seizures, and long-term damage to the mother's organs. The restricted blood flow has implications for the fetus as well: an inadequate supply of oxygen and nourishment means these babies tend to be small for their gestational age, and as the mother becomes more ill, they become listless.

Pre-eclampsia isn't exactly rare: about ten per cent of women develop elevated blood pressure in the latter phase of their pregnancies. Early-onset pre-eclampsia, which registers between week twenty, the halfway point of a pregnancy, and week thirty-two, the end of the seventh month, is far less common, and poses a more severe threat to both mother and baby. The warning signs — headaches, swelling, epigastric pain (often mistaken for heartburn) — are familiar to most pregnant women, but tend to be more extreme if a woman is pre-eclamptic. Then again, some women, like me, don't develop those warning signs at all, which makes this disease tricky to diagnose.

Untreated, the consequences of pre-eclampsia are dire: death for the baby, death for the mother. The only cure is to stop being pregnant. Babies who aren't yet severely compromised remain under surveillance in utero while the mother is given steroids to hasten the maturing of infant lungs. Others need to be delivered almost immediately. It's a knife-edge game: though the mother's body is normally the safest place for any pre-term baby, each day of restricted blood flow compromises a baby's growth and vitality.

I know almost none of this as I slide in and out of sleep all night. I have read the pregnancy handbooks, so I know that pre-eclampsia is a risk of pregnancy — and a slightly higher one for me having a first baby in my thirties. But the writers of these books downplay the dangers. They know that pregnant women are at the mercy of their bodies already, and often feel vulnerable and anxious. How could it benefit anyone to ratchet up the fear factor?

Statistics can be comforting. The chances of a first-time mother being stricken by early onset pre-eclampsia are slight, only about four chances in a thousand. What I realize, as I wrestle the night demons, is that some particular body, a real body, has to sit on the small side of that equation. That particular body is mine.

Wednesday, November 22, morning

WEDNESDAY DAWNS, AND NIGHT DREAD IS CROWDED OUT by the dull grind of illness. The blood pressure cuff is my constant companion, puffing up and releasing like a mechanical cobra. Doctors and nurses move in and out of my room, checking on the efficacy of various drugs.

I get an injection of steroids to hasten the baby's lung development. I understand that every intervention on the baby's behalf is essential, but I find it almost impossible to imagine what we're preparing for. Translating the secret, interior reality we've been sharing into the blunt actuality of birth seems inconceivable.

I'm not ready for this; my baby is not ready for this either. I want the next three months to prepare.

I feel dull from drugs and worry — but also because there's nothing really for me to do, apart from present my symptoms for management by expert others. One doctor breezes through and chides me for being in bed. I learn later that medical opinion is divided about prescribing bed rest for pre-eclamptic women — it can mask true blood pressure readings. At that moment, though, I feel stung, like she's implying that the concern that's circulating around and through me is excessive or contrived. I have no defence to wrap around me. She's the expert, I'm the problem.

Bill and I call our parents, all far away, and our closest friends, promise to keep them informed. As much as possible, we traffic in calm, a necessary counterpoint to the worry that burns through our news. Then we put our minds toward patching up the ragged ends of tasks abandoned at home — a couple of weeks of classes, a pile of marking, a conference for the graduate students in Bill's lab. We both feel so fortunate to have a strong network of friends and colleagues. They step into the absences we've left and take up responsibilities we don't even remember to consider. After the calls, we feel exhausted. We may have shared the weight, but now all of us feel helpless.

All through the night, nurses have cycled through, checking and checking. In the late morning, I meet one who sits at the end of my bed and really talks with me. Denise has the information I've been lacking. She explains the delicate decision-making that's already happening: my health is deteriorating, but at twenty-eight weeks, the odds of survival are not very high for the baby. When the detriments of disease outweigh the benefits of time, I'll be booked in for a Caesarean birth. She outlines the steps of the surgery. The anesthetist will inject drugs mid-spine to block feeling in the lower half of my body. The surgeon will make a low horizontal incision and deliver the baby. The neonatal care team will be standing ready to take the baby to the neonatal intensive care unit just down the hall. The doctor will remove the afterbirth and close up the incision, and I'll be wheeled into the recovery room. Bill will be present the whole time, and I'll have a nurse at my side.

I like this woman — there is something solid in her that cuts through the surreal haze of this experience. She doesn't pretend there is no risk, no pain, no terror. She expects I have the strength and the resources. I want to prove her right.

Wednesday, November 22, afternoon

PREPARATIONS QUICKEN. I'm moved over to a shared room on the maternity ward. Bill and I set out our few treasures, and send words to one another across the chasm of uncertainty. We're in unfamiliar territory now, we have to practise. My lunch tray arrives and my hunger surprises me. Bill steps out to find a sandwich.

He's barely back when a young woman shows up at the door, announces that the ultrasound technician is waiting for us. It's clear that we're late, though this is the first we've heard of this appointment. She turns on her heel and exits. I try to hurry but I am unsteady. I'm also overwhelmed with dread — I'm walking toward something I cannot fathom, something I cannot avoid. We train our eyes on the young woman disappearing ahead of us. I hold Bill's arm, swing one slippered foot past the other. I want to crumple into a pile here in this never-ending hallway, let all the feet pass. I want to resist this arrogant young woman; I want to refuse the demands of this story.

When we arrive at that crowded little closet, I heave my bulging self onto the table. The paper sheet complains under me, and the technician hovers, wand in hand, ready to plaster cold jelly onto my abdomen.

She writes whole paragraphs on my round drum. She never looks at her hand with its elaborate cursive movements — her attention is absorbed by the grey screen. She frowns, runs the wand back and forth, pressing and pausing, scribbling messages to herself. I have vanished for her: I am a cipher, a carrier of enigmas she is determined to unlock. I lie quietly, fighting my own trepidation. Her mouth purses tightly, she leans into the screen. She writes and writes, I am tethered to this moment, its sharp beak pressing into my flesh.

I open my mouth, find no words, close it again. I search for her eyes, but they have no interest in a fearful woman under a thin white sheet. They watch cloud formations on a monitor. I look at the screen too, but the foggy images have no meaning for me. *What can you see?* I ask tentatively. She doesn't answer right away — I am not her business. *The doctor will discuss it with you,* she says tersely.

My heart seizes. She won't speak because the baby is dead. She knows this awful thing and can't utter it. I want to leap from the table, tear my hair, scream my alarm to the far reaches of the earth. Instead, I tighten into stillness, an inhalation without relief. The paper under me absorbs an imprint of my swollen body, a disposable history of this moment. Apprehension, clutch of terror.

I will learn, soon, that she has not found a dead baby. But she is struck by the stillness of this little being. She counts movements — it takes a long time. What she sees on her cloud-watching expedition will alert the doctor: act swiftly.

Wednesday, November 22, evening

WHEN DENISE BOUNDED INTO MY ROOM late in the afternoon, she announced that they'd found a slot for my emergency surgery at 6:30. She was excited because she wouldn't have gone off-shift yet, and could attend at the delivery. I am flooded with gratitude — I feel stronger and safer with her nearby. As I will learn, it's one of the truths about serious illness: strangers become your intimates. Sometimes that proximity sturdies you, sometimes it injures you. For me, Denise is an ally, someone who sees through the complicated panic of this situation and finds me, a woman with fear, a woman with resources.

And now, for the first time in my conscious life, I'm in an operating room. It's cold in here; at least I'm cold. I'm nervous, too. What will it feel like to have a baby cut out of me? The room is white, bright, cluttered with its million unnamable instruments. I'm jittery, but I'm focusing on my tasks. I have to stay calm. In a way, staying calm is all I can offer my sick baby. It's precious little. Teetering on the lip of this enormous event, I'm determined to be present.

The anesthetist helps me heave my legs over the side of the bed. He asks me to curve out my spine and stay perfectly still. This part, I know, has its risks: all those prickly vertebrae evolved for a reason. He will ease his long needle between the bones, through the outer sheath and into the cord itself, numb sensation from mid-body down. A spinal block. I shiver with the chill of nerves, remind myself to breathe. *I can do this, I can do this.* I find myself whispering — this is my mantra, my participation in this inexorable story. The anesthetist hums country songs. The room is silent while he prepares.

Then Bill coos softly; his voice lifts me into my courage. I hunch over the inflated ball of my womb, opening up my back in readiness. Suddenly I have a vision of my grandmother with her dowager's hump. My grandmother: mother of thirteen, graceful in poverty and difficulty, a woman of generosity and fortitude. I push out my spine, connect myself to my mother, my mother's mother, to all the mothers. Our maternal bodies at the mercy of forces we'll never quite comprehend.

The drug slides in, I'm rolled back and strapped onto the bed. I'm relieved by the straps, to be honest: as the numbness spreads, I am losing my ability to balance. I can't feel myself. Or that's not quite true — I feel huge. I laugh up to Bill: *My legs are enormous, I have elephant legs!* He's at my head, determined protector, steely with intensity. He rests his hand on my shoulder, peers over the curtain that drapes across my chest.

The cast of characters is in place. Behind that curtain, act one is about to begin. I breathe awkwardly into the oxygen mask, gaze up. Denise is at one side, Bill at the other. We're set. I can feel pressure on my abdomen: *the incision*, I think. I'm uncomfortable, but I don't feel pain. The blood pressure cuff around my arm inflates frequently, and the punctures from yesterday's blood samples strangle and throb. I'm irritated by these intrusions — they distract me from the real event. I am inside now, willing my power into the small one who is about to make an entrance.

My chin begins to wobble violently, knocking my teeth against one another. I make an effort to relax myself. The banging stops, then starts again. I feel frustrated — obviously I'm not managing my nerves. Denise bends over, asks me again how I'm doing. *I can't stop my teeth from chattering,* I say. She smiles, squeezes my shoulder. *That's the drugs talking,* she says, *you can't do anything about that.*

She and Bill are increasingly absorbed in the process beyond the curtain. Later, Bill will say proudly that he's one of the only people who can say he loves me inside and out. *The layer of fat just under the skin is like a string of pearls,* he will say. I will be both repulsed and grateful. The abdominal pressure is taxing, perhaps because it is so abstract; I can't tell what is happening, or even where. I'm surprised by the whoop of excitement as the baby, a tiny girl, is lifted from my body. A huge hand holds her near my face for a brief moment before whisking her to the warming table and the ministrations of the NICU team.

She has pre-dawn eyes, deep blue and clear. She takes my measure as I take hers. We gaze across the gulf of air and challenge, assert our collective will. Both frail and tough, she is an ordinary miracle: a newly minted human. She is my daughter.

I laugh and cry, the world careens off its moorings, time stops to mark this arrival. My laughter silences, for a moment, the violence of my rattling teeth, the wheezing of the blood pressure cuff, the orchestrated movements of the many workers here. Bill has followed his daughter's magnetic trail to the warming table. Alone, strapped to this strange narrow table, I am released into my awe. A birth.

Denise leans down, quietly reviews the post-birth tasks with me: remove the placenta, repair the incision. The pressure is suddenly excruciating, and I feel nauseated by the heavy hands digging and digging. I am small and weak and worn out. It takes them forever to finish.

IN THE RECOVERY ROOM, Bill and I gaze at the Polaroid photo of our exquisite baby. We are awed by her steady gaze, the small rose of her lips. Denise, scrubbing alongside another nurse, remarks on her mouth, on the woolly halo of hair, the balance of her features. We are drunk on the photo. We look and look, try to comprehend the fact that this being, this extraordinary wee soul with her hat askance, has made us a family.

There's a carnival feeling in this room as the nurses wash up and put things in order. It feels odd to be in a bed parked in a room that's so unlike a resting place, and yet I am comfortable enough. The noise and chatter siphon away the tension of surgery. This is a time for joy — worry will come soon enough.

The nurses ask what we will name her. *Chloe*, we say with absolute confidence. We've carried this name for a few weeks, and she fit it beautifully when she arrived. Bill and I confer quietly, then ask Denise if we can give Chloe her name too. She blushes, sputters in surprise. *Chloe Denise*, our perfect baby.

Later I will discover that we've settled on names which mark out the reach of growth and chaos, the body in the world. Chloe means a *green shoot* — it reaches back to Demeter, the goddess of the green world. Denise comes from Dionysus, the god of ecstasy. It's a tall order for one small body to carry both growth and dissolution. Then again, it's the tall order we all face, the human challenge — painful, exhilarating, a whirl of flesh and dreaming.

The adrenalin of the occasion begins to fade and I sink toward exhaustion. Denise slips a needle into my intravenous line. *Morphine*, she whispers, *drug of choice. I'll check on you when I'm back in a couple of days. Rest and mend. You have a daughter!*

Thursday, November 23, morning

HOURS OR SECONDS LATER, I hear a voice through the murk. I try to hold it, but I can't make out the words. Everything is slick and brittle, I'm not quite here. A person moves nearby and I register the sound of curtains being pulled. The room bursts into brightness. Daytime, then. Thursday. I squint into the light. I don't know this room. Wait — yes, I was here before the surgery. I try to hold onto a thought. My brain is wispy, insubstantial.

Are you awake? she asks. This nurse is a patient woman, that's undeniable. I close my eyes, disappear, struggle again to the surface. She breezes about, checks my temperature, blood pressure, IV line, catheter. I watch, blinking: she is so quick, so accomplished. I work to hold that thought. It worries me, this thickness in my brain. Where have I gone?

Everything — is so — my thick tongue says carefully.

She turns toward me, pauses briefly. *What did you say?*

I — can't — every — second is — too —

I fall back toward the big silence. *How stupid,* I think, *that isn't right at all.* But I can't think what I might mean. I close my eyes. Consternation.

My eyes flick open. *It's the — drugs?* I'm flooded with relief. *I hate this — I've always —*

I scan the room, dogged by the suspicion that each thing slips out of its place just as my eyes sweep to the next thing. I am without anchor in a Dali landscape.

She listens to me blurt and stagger my way into consciousness. *I — hate this —* I say again. *I never —* I shake my head, try to clear some thinking space. *I can't —*

I am drawn to confess to her, this patient, sunny stranger, to apologize for my inadequacies. Though she won't remember this conversation, she offers me her generous smile, welcomes me back to the shared world. Then she is gone, moving out of orbit on those silent, competent shoes. The air currents eddy around my bed.

WHEN A NURSE SHOWS UP MID-MORNING, I am a little sharper. That's fortunate because she has plans: I am going to take my first steps. She begins by instructing me in the arcane details of the post-surgery dance. *Knees together, and push with the arms,* she says. *Good. Now, turn your whole body. Oh, don't twist your torso —*

My belly screams, my eyes roll back, I crash back into the pillows.

I'm stunned by the effort, to say nothing of the complexity, of simply rolling onto my side. The belly, I discover, is involved in everything: rolling, sitting, walking. Also breathing, groaning, weeping, speaking, laughing. I lie still. I don't want to move, that's the truth of it. My body is seized up in pain and anxiety. I'm no match for these twin companions, not today.

She puts her strong hand under my far shoulder. *Now then,* she says, *let's try that again.* It's a Herculean effort, but finally I am sitting. I'm pleased with myself, and now that the tensed muscles can relax, I'm almost comfortable. The world reorients itself, and for a moment I feel light. I could almost be happy here, legs loose in the unfamiliar air.

The nurse has other ideas. She explains that movement will speed my recovery — her voice perches between praise and scolding. *Okay*, she says, her voice hitching up the reins, *down you come.*

My arms push on the mattress, my feet stretch down to find the floor. My body howls: too much, too much. *Something will fall out,* I gasp. My hands jump, involuntary as birds, to cradle the injured belly. *Nothing must be lost,* I think, *nothing must be lost.*

I grip the nurse's arm, push one foot forward, then settle my weight on it. I'm a glacier, gravel grinds against me as I move. My belly screams. I glance down at the blue hospital gown, benignly stupid. It conceals a pending geyser of blood, I'm certain of it. I remind myself to breathe. Another step, another pause. I'm shaking from the effort. Pivot, pause, two steps back. I arrive back at the bed, rest my body against it a moment, begin the daunting task of climbing back in.

Tomorrow will be easier, the nurse says with conviction.

Thursday, November 23, afternoon

THE HOURS OF THURSDAY CRAWL BY, and I work to shake free of the drug haze. I'm rewriting the notion of confinement, I think in my lucid moments — I'm stranded in a hospital bed longing for an infant who is only hallways away but far beyond reach. I am thankful when Bill's face emerges into my barren hours, but he too is under siege, overtaken by a fear so fundamental it reframes his being. He brings me gifts: reports, numbers, tendencies, likelihoods. No matter how hard I listen, I can't quite hear what he is offering.

Every hour is a drama in Chloe's precarious life. Her unsuspecting body has come hurtling into a world of challenges. Breathing is a struggle; she needs the oxygen mask. A gavage tube snakes up her nose and into her stomach, carrying energy to fuel her body's effort. Heat to warm her tiny body rises up through the soft flannel under her. Breathing, feeding, staying warm: the daily work of being alive is an endless mountain-climbing expedition. That's all I know for certain, all I can grasp.

Life, for such a small and fragile being, is a series of small gains and terrifying eclipses. Or perhaps for her, life is only a series of taxing bewilderments. The people arrayed around the monitors celebrate the gains, hold their breath through the eclipses. We assign the meaning to the shape of this life — *she's making good strides, she's having more difficulty* — and invest ourselves in the version of a future we are obliged to choose. Each time you enter the NICU, you pass a wall of pictures, photos of the children who've blossomed from the other distressed seeds who once lived here. It's possible; it happens all the time.

I participate in this dream, of course I do. I celebrate the doctors with their gentle hands, their extraordinary skills. I celebrate the nurses who stand guard, day and night, their gestures shaping a life lived with unremitting intensity. I sit in my room, dreaming of a child who will romp across the pastures of my childhood, flop down in dandelions so thick they carpet the world yellow.

I dare to hope, but I dread that hope too. *What if she dies?* That's the question that hangs like attic dust in the air, the question that neither Bill nor I can speak, the question that suffocates our friends, our families. Unspoken but present, it frightens us out of our wits.

Another question hangs like a wraith behind that one: *What if she needs to die and can't find her way?* It haunts me, but I know I will never place it in anyone's ear.

Hi, Mom?

Hello, honey. I've been waiting to hear from you. How are you?

Okay, I think. No — actually, no. I don't know.

I'm awake again, and the room is painfully bright, sun streaming across the covers of my bed. The time is out of joint, as Hamlet would say: the sky should be lowering, reflecting back my clouds of tension. My belly is a mutiny of damaged muscles. It takes practice to remember to move with your arms.

Um, Mom? I need you to come.

I wondered if you'd like me there. I'll call the travel agent's office, get things arranged. I should be there tomorrow or the next day.

I have been untied from my life, my ravaged body beached here in this sun-drenched nightmare. Dread is my ghost.

Mom? I need you to come now. I'm not sure —

I'll call now. I'll be there as soon as I can.

My mother, my mother. She will comfort me. She will wrap her strength around me, soothe me through my nightmare.

Sorry, Mom. I know it's awkward —

Don't worry, honey. Just hold on: I'll be there soon.

Sun. Fear. Yearning.

Mom? Thanks. I love you. Give my love to Dad.

We love you too.

EVEN THOUGH I AM SWALLOWING CLUSTERS OF PILLS every few hours, my blood pressure continues to spin out of control. My abdomen screams, my head aches, I am shaky from the morphine — I feel grim. Still, my desperation to be with my baby overpowers my ravaged body. Bill helps me navigate five excruciating steps to the wheelchair, then wheels me through a maze of hallways to the neonatal unit. He has spent the night at

Chloe's isolette, and the morning hours too. His human physiology training gives him an unusual comfort in this place — he asks intelligent questions of the care team, adds his energy to theirs. He is not put off by the machines and noise. *It's a place that never sleeps,* he tells me, and I can feel the awe in him.

It's not so much the activity I dread, but the formality, the necessary distance that fragile health dictates. This is a baby I will be able to look at but not hold, a baby who is cared for by people who know better than I how to meet her needs. My relief and gratitude have a bitter aftertaste.

Bill leads me through the scrub routine: there's a hand-washing protocol, then we don gowns and slippers. I'm grateful to have him as my guide. I am a stranger, but already he moves with assurance. The wheelchair is awkward, bumping through the swinging doors into this crowded room. He's right — it is a noisy place, well-lit and intensely busy. We wind through the maze of isolettes, and we're there. The circle of caregivers shifts to accommodate us. Bill helps me stand, introduces me to the team, then turns his attention to the monitors to see how Chloe is faring.

I hardly register the names of the doctors and nurses — I am compelled only by this baby they attend to. I want to absorb everything about her, everything about this moment, this place. I commit her to memory there in her present home, an open isolette warmed from beneath and ringed by monitors and attentive faces. In the top corner sits the floppy-eared bunny, at the bottom, a sign — Chloe Denise — lettered on the back of a warranty card by a friend who made the midnight drive to support the new father.

I sink into the look of this lovely child, my own daughter. She is narrow, and red as raw salmon. I see her strong limbs, determined face, long feet and hands, feathery hair like flames from a black sun. Tubes snake into her nose, and IV lines are taped to her body. She is small, only about as long as my forearm, but she commands her space and the attention of the people gathered around her. She is powerful, she is compelling. And she is absolutely separate from me.

She is also very busy. I can feel her, mounting her own resistance against the possible influx of blood that could drown her tiny lungs. Being alive is work, hard work. I shudder to think how the tube in her nose and the IV lines in her feet and scalp must have hurt on entry — an unwelcome welcome to the world.

I gaze and gaze, even as my own body begins to crumple from the effort of being upright. I tunnel deep into this exact moment, my witness to this determined, passionate spirit. Then I collapse into the wheelchair and Bill wheels me back to my room. I struggle up onto my bed and fall back against the pillows. When I close my eyes, I can see my beautiful, challenged baby. Someone in that relentlessly busy unit pasted hearts onto the monitors taped to her tiny chest. I am struck dumb by that small and very human gesture.

Thursday, November 23, evening

AS DARKNESS FALLS on our first full day as a family, Chloe crosses a momentous line: at twenty-four hours, her chances of survival improve dramatically. Bill sits at the edge of my bed and reports that the NICU team is jubilant. It amazes me to think that people who were strangers to us yesterday have invested so much of themselves in our baby. They have allied themselves with her stubborn will to live — her life *matters* to them. I am thankful, I am relieved, but I am not quite strong enough to celebrate. I am haunted by dark futures, dizzied by the precariousness of this three-legged waltz.

Around midnight, my mom arrives. She enters my room and it calms me immeasurably. She sits next to me and strokes the hair back from my face. I tell her where I am, where I've been, where I might be going. We talk quietly in the dark. She soothes her adult child, and I find my way toward sleep.

Friday, November 24

BY THE TIME DAYLIGHT ANNOUNCES FRIDAY, I am nearly blinded by the ache in my head. The nurses wheel my bed into a single room just off the nursing station so they can keep an eye on me. They bring in a cot for Mom.

The doctors come and go, check my vitals, register their concern about this pain. I see them wondering if it's psychosomatic — I wonder that myself, lying in my dim room. Could a person invent pain to protect her from being with a sick baby? Could a headache like this be fashioned from dread? I haul myself into a sitting position, guilty and anxious, and will myself to make the trek to the NICU. But I am no match for this headache. Before I get settled in the wheelchair, I am overcome, and have to lay myself down again.

Time is stretched by effort. I can't bear light, I can't bear noise. Mom closes the curtains against the wan November light, sets the photo of Chloe in amongst the first bouquets of flowers on my bedside table. Friends begin to call, and a few drive down to offer support and share worry. Mom intercepts them in the hallway, brings their care back to me in small pieces.

She spends a few minutes with Chloe, then comes back to lay a cool cloth on my forehead. She shares her visit to the NICU, she offers news from home, she tells me stories from my childhood. She moves around the room, her pendant chiming gently in the low light. When I can't settle, she reads to me. Though I am too ill to concentrate, I can hear, and the contours of her voice are as familiar as childhood. I follow her soothing trails through pain-addled hours.

The nurses and doctors begin to speculate that I might be suffering from a spinal headache, one of the risks associated with the spinal block procedure. Occasionally the needle which channels the numbing drugs into the body leaves a perforation of the dura, a membrane within the spinal column, and the spinal fluid leaks out. When the body is upright, the fluid drains down, leaving the brain scraping against the bony skull. Spinal headaches are not common — about one chance in two hundred — and will often correct themselves with a couple of days of bed rest. The alternative to waiting is a procedure called a blood patch: the anesthetist deposits a few drops of blood at the injured site where they can form a scab, stopping the leak.

The doctors are uncertain. My blood pressure is not only elevated, but also resistant and hard to control. The medication is aggressive, so perhaps that's the culprit. There's no shortage of emotional challenge in my present situation, no doubt that's contributing. A blood patch has its own risks, so they're reluctant to order one until the picture is clearer. They make notes, consider options.

All I know is that I am being levelled by a steamroller. This headache is enormous, unthinkable. It crowds out every other sensation. A Polish doctor arrives unannounced, offers to share her training in acupuncture. I feel the million hair-pokes in my back and legs, and fall deeply asleep. My mother sighs with relief, steps out for a walk in the fresh air. An hour later when I awake, the headache is back, grinding away. We both sag with disappointment.

I lean toward my struggling daughter, mere minutes from my room. A universe of illness divides me from my life. I am pinned to my bed, an aching body huddled in a nest.

My mother attends to me.

WITH HIS UNUSUAL MIX OF TENDERNESS AND TRAINING, Bill is better at finding his place in an NICU than most first-time fathers. All his years of anatomy and physiology study arrange themselves into an elaborate mosaic around that tiny isolette, and he assumes his position, a passionate man keeping vigil.

He gets to know the team who care for Chloe. He has tremendous respect for Dr Shah and Dr Schmidt, her primary neonatologists. They are intense, meticulous, decent. They involve him in their decision-making, honour his connection to this small being. They also care — about the baby, about him, about the demands these difficult circumstances make on all of the people circled around this baby. He meets Helen, the NICU social worker, who impresses him with her warmth and sensitivity. She feels like an ally, someone who knows where he is.

He shares time and tasks with a constellation of neonatal nurses. They answer his million questions, map the experience in their hands onto the knowledge in his brain. They interpret the readings on the machines, they explain the outcomes of their various interventions. They also urge him to go for walks, for food, for sleep. Mostly he will refuse. Occasionally, he will grab a coffee and a misshapen sandwich from the canteen downstairs and then drop in on me, speedy with adrenalin, as he returns to the unit. One nurse threatens to evict him from the NICU if he doesn't go away and take a proper sleep — after all, there are sleeping rooms in this hospital for family members like him. He is so afraid of her that he actually sleeps for five hours straight.

He is compelled, driven. He has exchanged roles with me and will be present for this baby now, the way I have been present all the other days of her life. If you asked him, he couldn't articulate this need. It possesses him, he's in its thrall.

When the intensity around Chloe's isolette becomes overwhelming, he redirects his worry, cutting snowflakes and linked people from coloured paper he buys at the drugstore downstairs. I will tease him about his decorating style. We will smile toward one another, flinching away from the pain of it. *I needed to — it's her only home right now*, he will say.

Friday, November 24, afternoon

BY AFTERNOON, I REALIZE THIS HEADACHE is not about to subside. *When I sit up, it's like my brain is rasping on concrete*, I tell Bill when he stops by. I am lying back in the stillness of my room, and I've had a good rest. I muster my determination: I want to go back to the NICU with him.

I struggle into the chair and he takes me swiftly through the halls. *Hurry*, I mutter, my desperation rising with the whine of the headache. *Hurry — I can't sustain this for long...* We arrive and scrub, then burst through the doors. Bright lights, noise, and inside my skull, the shrill screech of pain. We arrive at the isolette and I haul myself up. My eyes fill with this perfect baby, this tiny intense being. She is naked, her hands fisted, her eyes closed under the burden of work. Her bed shakes gently, a strategy her team initiated yesterday to help break up the fluids challenging her immature lungs. I take her in — desperate mother, valiant daughter. She is beautiful, utterly and spectacularly beautiful.

I begin to crumple. Bill eases me back into my chair and we race back through the hallways. I must be prone — it's an imperative yelling through every cell in my body. By the time we reach my room, I am spent and weeping. My mother and my partner lift my aching body onto the bed and release me into rest.

I WAKE UP EXHAUSTED. Mom tells me that Helen, the neonatal social worker, has come by to see me, and will return before she goes off-shift. I can see that she is pleased, but I am too weary and demoralized to want to meet anyone else. No matter what the angle, nothing is good about our situation: my baby is facing inhuman demands just to stay alive, all of us are desperate with worry, and today's excursion confirms beyond doubt that I am too ill to visit her. Talking can't change anything — I don't want to talk.

I take my pills, I drink my water, I fuss. I lever my body off the bed and make the agonizing trek to the bathroom, then return to collapse against the pillows. Even with the curtains drawn, my eyes ache from the light.

By the time Helen arrives, I've stopped feeling petulant — I'm too taxed by physical demands to maintain a decent pout. She's clearly happy to see Mom, and then shines her attention toward me as she settles into a chair. Right away I see she's not the person I expected. There's no determined helpfulness in her, no trace of patronizing advice-giving that would indicate she's watched our particular trauma play itself out over and over. She's direct, calm, curious, concerned. Also, it strikes me, joyful. The air in my room feels lighter.

Helen sits with us in the late afternoon. She shares her wonder in my daughter. *Such a fiery spirit,* she says, *a remarkable little being.* She speaks about Bill too, his strength and kindness, his passionate attachment to his daughter. She overheard one of the nurses say that in all her years in the NICU she has never met a better father. She asks me about my challenged body, shakes her head with concern. *I can imagine that not being well enough to visit must be tying you up inside,* she says. *At this point, regaining your health has to be your priority. Your wonderful mom will help you, and we will stand near your beautiful daughter until you can join her. You will be there soon enough...*

Saturday, November 25, morning

THE NURSE IN THE DOORWAY Saturday morning is one I haven't encountered before. I can't decipher her enthusiasm, can't tell if she knows everything or nothing about me. She's pointing out that I should begin expressing milk for my baby — breast milk is ideally constituted, the perfect baby food. I know all this, but find myself completely confounded. I can't even get my damaged self down the hallways to see my baby struggling in NICU, let alone imagine, so many weeks shy of my due date, nursing her. I haven't read those chapters yet — I'm not ready.

I look back at her, perplexed.

She doesn't miss a beat. She will teach me to use the electric breast pump. It may take a while to stimulate milk production, but whatever I can produce, even if it's only a few drops, will be frozen and stored, ready for the moment my baby is strong enough to take food. She stands in the doorway, expectant.

I can't imagine any of it: the moment of production, the moment of consumption.

Then again, a maternal body is a responsible body, and pumping milk gives me a tangible way to help this baby who is so present and so distant. My mom helps me into the wheelchair and pushes me down the hall. It occurs to me that I will feel shy and awkward with this competent stranger. It doesn't occur to me that pumping milk will be physically and emotionally painful.

I seat myself in the silent, lamp-lit room. The woman describes the parts of the contraption on the cart in front of me, and I force myself to listen. The monster and I look at one another suspiciously. The nurse fits the suction cup over my unpractised breast, instructs me to reduce the suction to the lowest setting. Then she flips the switch and the machine wheezes to life. My nipple leaps into the suction cup, I flinch in surprise. I hear the pump sucking and sighing, and suddenly I am transported to the dairy barn of my childhood, cows lined up, glancing over their flanks, chewing.

It's the indignity, I suppose, and the discomfort. Even though I will learn to use the pump, bracing myself for the first bloom of breast pain, I will never forgive its cool detachment. It doesn't care that priming milk out of unready breasts is a taxing exercise. It doesn't care that I am expressing milk for a baby who may never drink it. It's a machine — it cannot fathom the intimacy of nourishing a baby.

Because I am so ill, my first lesson is short. I am relieved to escape: I need to think this through, to make my peace with the cows, with the insolent heap of metal.

When I return a few hours later, the nursing room, thankfully, is still empty and together my mom and I tackle the machine. *What does this switch do again? Does this part hook in there?* My breasts shrink away from the task, but I'm more determined than they are.

Suctioning both breasts at once, the nurse has pointed out, is the most efficient; I'm persuaded by the logic and eager to complete this mission. Arrange, position, squeeze, hold. Flick the switch. Sharp intake of breath: my nipples jump away from my body, threaten to disappear up the flexible tubing. The machine grinds away, oblivious. *I hate this machine*, I mutter.

I'm awkward, two hands holding two suction cups to two forlorn breasts. I look at my mom. She looks back, caught between distaste and pity. I moo. We're both taken aback; I can't believe I've done that, wonder if I've disgraced myself and my absent daughter. Then suddenly we're laughing madly, both of us, a pair of children mooing at an ugly machine. My head pounds. A bead of fluid blooms from my left nipple.

Over the next couple of days, this machine will drag from me only minuscule amounts of colostrum, the rich first milk the nurses call liquid gold. I will wonder, as I face an apparently endless parade of straws each day, *how is it possible to drink three gallons of water and produce three drops of milk?*

But I will also combat a cloying sense of failure, and an irrational fear that placing those vials, identified by name and date, into the freezer is somehow tempting fate. I try to stay positive, but the thought of those vials being orphaned plagues my dreams.

SATURDAY AND SUNDAY — my fourth and fifth days in this hospital — crawl past, narrowed by intensity and illness. I am anchored by my own pain and the dread-filled distance from my daughter. I drink my water, I take the containers of pills that battle my blood pressure, I doze to escape the shrieking headache. I dream of relief, but I hardly dare imagine it: a robust baby, a return of my own good health, a release from this harrowing storyline.

The hours are punctuated by doctors and nurses on their rounds. Bill comes by to check in every three hours or so, Mom visits Chloe when I rest. I have never been so incapacitated — I can hardly shuffle eight steps to the bathroom, and I have perhaps three minutes in a sitting position before I am crushed by the pain in my head.

My room continues to fill with flowers. Mom reads me letters and cards, relays news to and from the world outside the hospital walls. I can feel the life in the people around me — husband, mother, this community of care providers, and beyond them our friends and family — but it is far from me, separate, apart. I am in another realm. I am eager for reports of the spirited battle going on in the NICU, and I am swamped with gratitude for the brave father who is there by proxy for me too. I can feel his worry about me, but we both know it's not the time for that. He is doing our work, releasing me to slog through illness.

One of our friends has delivered a package from my first-year English class. They met just about the time my baby was delivered, and the sign-in sheet transformed itself into a missive as it passed from desk to desk. My mom reads their names and messages in my hushed room, and I think about who they are, so vivid in the first bloom of adulthood. Some admit they're missing my flamboyant maternity clothes or tease me about choosing an extreme excuse to skip class. Others are unsettled, share cautious concern. A few disengage completely, signing only their names.

From their angle, I am young enough that they can feel the heat I leave along the path. Many of them will have their own babies in the next few years, and now I am an example they don't particularly want to acknowledge. I'm not so comfortable here either: I have been catapulted into the covert category of ill mothers and fragile infants, the limbo world of potential mourners.

The plain truth for us all is that my baby could die. Every hour of her life settles like a dusting of snow on the bedrock of that knowledge. I wonder if I could bear the death of my own child. I wonder how a person could possibly prepare for a loss of that magnitude. I gather around me the encouraging notes from my students, the expressions of concern from friends and family. I feel the whole network of effort willing this baby to survive. I am so thankful to belong to all these people, yet even banded together, our force is small.

I lean toward my baby in the NICU. I conjure the team of experts around her, so lavish with their attention, their skills, their compassion. My baby could die. Today, tomorrow, next week, next month, next year. One day she will die — that's part of the script that began when she began.

One day. But not now, not this minute.

Sunday, November 26, afternoon

SUNDAY. WATER SHEETS OVER MY BODY, I am lost in the glory of the heat, the watery massage to damaged skin and muscles. This is my first shower in days, and I huddle on the stool in the tiled enclosure, curled around my abdomen's mad march of staples, elbows propped on knees.

My mother stands on the other side of the narrow doorway, watching me in my watery cocoon. She is concerned, but she sets that aside. We're a team, and we're on a mission: I need a shampoo.

Already I'm exhausted. The effort to get here and then to sit down on this stool has nearly bested me—I cannot possibly reach up and detach the telephone shower, lather and rinse my wasted body. I glance at my mom; her eyes are far from here. The headache shrieks for attention, but I pull into myself, listen to the pelting water. My body would stay forever in this flood. If I knew how, I would will myself to leach away: disappearance, transformation.

I look again toward my mom, see her taking stock. She is determined to respect my privacy and independence, but she also knows how to help. We are exploring new territory together: she is finding the mother in her daughter.

She hesitates, pushes up her sleeves, then slips off her shoes and socks, rolls up her pant legs, and steps over the lip of the doorway into this sodden world. Co-conspirators, we grin at one another. She is my Huckleberry Finn, suddenly jaunty, even shy. She takes the water in her hands, spills ache and sorrow over my spine, down my calves, off the bones at my wrists. She lathers me, gentle hands on a beloved and still-familiar body, and I am her child again, lapped in a mother's attention.

Shortly, I will be back in the wheelchair, clean and moaning for my bed. My mother, steady and clear, will steer me down a hallway of identical doors. Her shoes will be dry, her pant legs will have migrated to their proper length. Nobody will know her river journey.

MY ROOM IS AN ARBOUR, the thick smell of lilies and roses a curtain to pass through. Everyone remarks that the flowers are amazing. They are. Close by, I keep the vase of large white lilies, a cluster of shooting stars. In my room are perfect ivory roses too, and daisies and mums and freesia and whispery things I don't recognize. Every flower has been cradled in someone's hands. Each one has been chosen specifically, and placed into visual conversations that require no words from me. They release me into the quiet of my listening.

The flowers crowded into my room teach me about serenity. They are quietly separate from my wracked body, my anxious bewilderment over the sick baby I can't even visit. They shine in the low light of my room, and soothe me with their uncomplicated beauty, their generosity.

I am grateful for the flowers. They sing me through the death terror that hovers near me, hour by hour — not only the possible death of my baby who fights every minute for the air in her lungs, but the death that belongs to us all, our dissolution or release, the absolute mystery that awaits us. The threat of death looms near me in the abbreviated November days, but the flowers, severed from their roots and staging elegant deaths, show me that dread has no real place here. Not here, not anywhere. I may counter with hope, prayer, bargains, rage, but what happens next isn't for me to say. Living and dying are what living beings do, have always done. When death arrives, it will require us to pay our observances, then it will move on and leave us to find our way through the shattered landscape.

The flowers in my room carry the print of the people who've sent them, people who have arrayed themselves around us in our time of terrible need. But mostly the flowers register the thick sweep of living things, the barrage of beauty and spirit that animates the world. Their dusky smell tells me I'm home. I, too, am destined to bloom and die.

Monday, November 27, afternoon

A BRAIN-ACHE HIJACKS YOU, flies you far from yourself and into a miasma of pain. Three days, four days, five — time is elastic when a body is in distress. When the doctors decide to schedule a blood patch for Monday afternoon, Mom and Bill are visibly relieved. I am almost too exhausted to feel hopeful. I am wheeled into the prep room, and lie on my gurney. The wait is long, or perhaps it is not. I wake, I doze, I wake again. I am desperate for relief, but I no longer have the energy to be impatient. All of us in this hospital need attention — waiting is what we do.

When I finally am wheeled into the theatre, nervous and fragile, I am surprised to see the same anesthetist. I liked him from the start — his manner in the delivery room, off-hand and witty, is sharp in my memory. Just like that, I am released from being merely a woman suffering a headache to a woman who has experienced the momentousness of a birth. I feel lifted up.

He reaches toward me, rests his hand on my shoulder. *I have never had trouble with that needle,* he says. *I'm so surprised — I'm so sorry.* Another compassionate stranger, his sympathy almost makes me weep. He explains the procedure briefly: he will draw a few drops of my blood, then slide the needle between the bones of my spine and deposit them at the site of the spinal block. The blood will form a scab, and if what I'm suffering is a spinal headache, the leakage will stop. When the spinal fluid is restored, my brain will be properly cushioned and the throbbing will subside.

We settle into the task at hand. It's painful, yes, but blessedly brief. Then he squeezes my shoulder again, wishes me a fast recovery, and disappears into the fray. I feel wretched, but I feel hopeful too. It's a welcome change.

The recovery room is like a summer camp gone wrong — dozens of beds with moaning bodies, perky nurses weaving through, checking and charting. I withdraw, will myself to become invisible in this public zone.

A blood patch? the nurse sings out, glancing at my chart. *Oh, you've had a baby then!*

I gasp. She knows only what is printed on that paper, but I am stunned by how invasive her question feels, how callous. I retreat into myself. I have had a baby, yes, a small, perfect baby who is near me and far from me, climbing the mountains of her own little life.

I'm suddenly furious: I don't want anything to do with any of them — their can-do attitudes, their casual trespasses. I don't want to be parked here in this muttering sea of illness, aching and fearful and exhausted.

I feel exposed, my skin pried back, the heart's muscle leaping away in surprise. Stranded on the bed, I will the minutes to pass so I can be wheeled back to safety.

Tuesday, November 28, morning

I SLEEP FOR HOURS, Monday evening and all through the night, my body working to restore itself. When Tuesday dawns, the headache has cleared. After days of unremitting pain, this release is a miracle: I can raise my exhausted body into an upright position, I can take a few steps on my own without collapsing, I can talk, I can breathe, I can think. I'm weak and unsteady, but at least I can imagine my way toward the next hour. I am flooded with relief.

Everyone is excited for me. Finally I will be able to join the brigade of watchers at the edge of Chloe's isolette. Six days. She has navigated six precious, demanding, miraculous days. By all accounts she is stronger after so many storms. Each one brings us all closer to hope and expectation.

I align myself with this fighting spirit. At the same time, it shames me to know that I am afraid of the place she lives, afraid of the demands it places upon our human need to reach one another. I fear I will fail at this version of mothering. I have missed her life with its hushed moments and command performances. I know only her eyes, her narrow, red body — I'm not sure that is enough.

Mom takes me to the NICU in a wheelchair. I compose myself, breathe into my anxiety. We scrub, then enter the bustle of attention. I feel I'm intruding, though the strangers around Chloe's isolette welcome me warmly, reshape the circle to include me. I gaze at the red baby, wonder that she could be mine. Hands move deftly around her body, attending to lines and wires. They wave invisible magic wands, dare the impossible. I am mesmerized by the bewildering fact of this child's life.

Voices circle around me. I struggle to grasp the details of improving health, of amazing resilience. I am absorbed by this baby, this stubborn, determined baby. My hand slips toward hers, nestles against her tiny fingers. I long to know this child, to take her into myself. I long to be her mother.

I lean my broken body toward her, my magnetic north, and begin to sing. I fold my voice into the smallest envelope, send it through the relentless beeping and buzzing of the machines in this space, the rustle of hands and shoes and clean smocks. I sing through my fingertip, send waves up her bruised arm. I am determined to find her. I am seeking her heart, sending an ancient love letter from mother to daughter. I sing her my astonishment, my anguish, my apologies. I sing her my hope, I sing her my dread, I sing her my blessing. I sing her a mother.

THE CAREGIVERS AROUND CHLOE have shared their optimism and confidence, but I sense something else, a pending change in the weather. Then this small being arches her back, and concern telepaths around the isolette. The nurse looks at me pointedly and declares that Chloe can't handle extra stimulation.

I am aghast. My voice ties itself into a knot at the back of my throat. I pull my hand away, and remove myself from the circle. This is a place for the medical team who knows this baby's body so intimately. It is not a place for a longing mother.

I close my eyes against the tubes and wires invading her body, the effort of breathing. These crests of danger have shaped her days, and the days of her caregivers, since she was born. Where is my place? This is not mothering as I've imagined it. I wonder if I have the stamina.

I stand back and watch my baby's heavy work. Then my mother wheels me back to my room. I weep silently through the maze of hallways.

Tuesday, November 28, afternoon

BACK IN MY ROOM, I TAKE ANOTHER CLUTCH OF PILLS, have some food, remind myself that this crisis is one of many. We're running a marathon rather than a sprint — we all need to manage our energy reserves. Mom heads to the NICU so that Bill can make a quick trip to the cafeteria. I do my best to rest. Despite my resolve, I can feel the dreads taking over. I'm like a child falling down a well. I wait for Bill to swing by with his lunch. He will put solid ground under me again.

A stranger's head leans in the door, announces that Chloe's distress is intensifying, then disappears. Suddenly, I am frantic. I struggle into the wheelchair. When Bill appears a minute later, we race across to the NICU. Now panic is my demon-partner; it steals my breath, bangs my heart. We race through the scrub-in, find our way through the maze to Chloe's isolette. The doctors and nurses cluster, each person drilled to the task at hand. Skill, intuition, determination: their hands flit like strung birds above the labouring baby. I watch, stunned by fear.

Dr Jay pulls back, turns his body to locate us. His eyes announce the severity of this moment. *This is our preparation*, I think, but I can't imagine what is next. He steps over to us, explains that Chloe has internal bleeding which is not responding well to their interventions. The situation is critical. He disappears into the dance of arms.

He emerges again, moments later, comes swiftly to speak to us: *She's bleeding, her lungs, I don't think she can make it through —*

His voice, his hands: he holds us to him, speaks to our deeper selves. We nod, dumbly, lean into his compassion.

We can continue if that's your choice, he says, *but I really think —*

The air drains from the room. Now I truly am falling down the well. I hear the echo of damp brick walls, feel the splash of water below me. I will go down, down. I will never move out of this deep place. Nothing will reach me. I will die, slowly, at the bottom of my sorrow.

No —

We speak simultaneously, our voices startle us.

Don't prolong — If — No —

There are no words to initiate death. We fashion our ache from silence, relieved by its sturdiness, its subtlety.

His hands, mourning doves, settle on our shoulders. He stands with us, quiet, respectful.

Do you want to hold the baby? he asks.

My back hunches up to save my heart from a hurt it cannot sustain. The arms above the isolette change their choreography. They swiftly detach the array of wires and tubes, unplug the red body. Bill circles his arms around me, and together we reach and reach, we reach to hold our dying daughter.

We stand, Bill and I, circled into one another, enveloping our baby. Someone leads us, gently, to the room at the edge of the NICU, the quiet room. My mother follows us. The air is blue, dense and still. We ease our bodies into the soft furniture, practise the feel of arms around her failing body. She spans the length of my forearm, palm to elbow. She is small, but she is definite. We are struck by the potency of her, the strength of muscles exercised by pain, the perfect definition of her parts.

It occurs to me, suddenly, that I have never been in the presence of a dead person. Will I be afraid? Will I be sickened? I feel awkward and stupid, inept, ashamed. I stammer my apprehension and pass through the wave of fear. Then we sit in silence, awed by the passage. The child, this utterly beautiful girl child, settles softly in my arms; her father reaches around us both, holding us to him. Her little heart stops — at some point her heart stops — and we continue to sit, an aching family in an impossible embrace.

DEATH IS WHAT IT IS: A QUIET, MYSTICAL CATACLYSM. We sit in the blue light, weep and wonder, speak gently into the velvet air. It's a physical relief to have her tiny body in contact with my body. I feed the deep reaches of my belly with breath. We define a shape for our family in these moments of holding, we claim her body for our own.

Minutes pass, maybe hours, and I am surprised by the intensity of the calm here at this point of catastrophe. Something leaves, and our wishful selves fly after it. But something stays too, something clear and ringing, something indelible. I will spend my life discovering what it is, this deep, true thing.

IT'S HARD TO SAY, EXACTLY, WHEN A DEATH IS FINISHED. The
doctors and nurses come, by ones or twos, carrying their pain and
defeat awkwardly. They sorrow for us, but they also sorrow for
themselves.

They come and sit with us, these exhausted, compassionate
people, and we are quiet together in the blue light. Everything has
imploded into this minute, this space: the world is here, circling
around this child's small, cooling body. We nourish ourselves in
the calm, prepare for the long climb out of the well.

AT SOME POINT, WE ARE SPENT FROM THE WORK OF ATTENTION.
A nurse lifts Chloe, small treasure, from our arms, and we make
our way back to my room. We are mostly numb. Shock is a natural
anesthetic, that's part of it, but also this revision of our reality is so
profound that we no longer quite know who we are. It takes clarity
to perceive what is broken.

Helen comes with us, I'm glad of that. We are walking
through a new land, and she is a steadying guide. We enter the
profusion of flowers and I am suddenly exhausted and fragile. I
need medication. I need rest. My body is not sturdy.

I collapse into my bed. Bill perches on the edge, takes
my hand. Helen pulls a chair alongside us. *Where's Mom?* I say,
suddenly anxious. *I thought she was with us.* My mother — I can
feel her imprint in that quiet room with the dying baby, her imprint
here in my room too, caring for me through the long hours of
illness.

She stayed behind, Helen says. *She has her own messages for
that little granddaughter. It's important, Charlene — and no, she's
not alone.*

I think of my mom braving her way through these days of
mothering me through my pain, and weaving the fiery spirit of this
granddaughter into her life story too. She and Dad know better

than almost anyone what it means to agonize over a fragile baby: their first child was born with spina bifida, and lived on love and determination for almost a year, months longer than anyone had predicted. They were young when they crashed into her death. I have the advantage of ten more years of living, and of parents who have walked this path ahead of me.

Helen and Bill and I let the afternoon settle around us. We talk, we weep, we tell each other small stories. Helen answers our questions, but mostly she shows us what we carry forward. Chloe's life was brief but her days do have their narratives of triumph and connection. We have a cast of people who have brought their skills and their passion to the aid of a struggling infant, and to her mother as well. We have our families, and we have our friends, all of them ringed around us. We have one another, and we have ourselves. *You are strong*, she says.

She looks around my room. *The flowers here are beautiful,* she says. We gaze at the riot of blossoms, breathe in the scent.

Her voice becomes gentle. *Walking into an empty house can be a very painful moment for parents who've lost a baby,* she says. *You will find many ways to bring Chloe home, but you might begin by carrying in an armful of flowers.*

Tuesday, November 28, evening

THE AFTERNOON FLOATS BY. Mom and Bill each go off to make the first painful calls, unleashing our sorrow into the bigger world. I can feel all of our people, staggering with the weight of it. Nurses move through my haze, checking my recovery — with my daughter no longer here to anchor us, they are anxious for me to be well enough to leave. We all feel the press for privacy.

My room is a sanctuary in the falling darkness. Released from clock and calendar, Mom and Bill and I drift in this swirling, sorrowing present. The flowers accompany us. Eventually Bill climbs into bed beside me, Mom stretches out on her cot, and we allow our exhausted bodies to rest.

Wednesday, November 29, morning

THE MORNING IS A BLUR of final visits from doctors, and arrangements for my discharge. Helen, clear-headed and compassionate, helps us think through all the complex decisions that attend a death — the question of autopsy, and the possible futures for the small broken body resting I have no idea where. I put my mind to each of these things, but abstractly — I'm a chilled amphibian.

Sometime mid-morning, I look at Helen across the wide, cold valley, and wonder how I can possibly go back into a classroom. I feel my students with their intent faces, I feel the effort it takes to animate the conversations that happen in those classrooms. I can't imagine where that energy would come from — I can't imagine caring enough to find it. *I don't see how I can do it,* I say.

You don't. She says it simply, then pauses, reading the electricity in the room. *Take your maternity leave, Charlene. Find your way through your sorrow, then do whatever is next. You'll know.*

I'm startled. It hasn't occurred to me that a woman with no baby could take maternity leave. It's a conundrum that exceeds semantics: am I a mother if I have no child?

As the morning ends, Bill goes off to face the horror of a nearby funeral chapel. The trite river scene in the entrance offends him, as does the programmed sympathy of the chapel director. No one can fathom the loneliness, the exhaustion, the distress in this bereaved man. We have settled on cremation — Bill sets his jaw and picks through the details for a fire he can't bear to consider.

I'm relieved that he's clear, decisive, able to act on our behalf. I have some inkling of the cost.

In his absence, I gather my few things. For the first time in days, I put on real clothes. I'm alone, and testing the experience. Mom has gone down to the drugstore to find a journal she saw a few days back. I expect she has taken a walk outside as well — she will be desperate for some space for her own sorrow.

I roll my bed into the upright position, eat my lunch, doze away the minutes. I am, I think, ready to go home. I imagine the quiet there, both solace and reproof.

Wednesday, November 29, afternoon

FIVE OR SIX PEOPLE, maybe more, suddenly break through my veil of waiting. I feel a clutch of anxiety, then recognize a few of their faces. Dr Shah, Chloe's gentle, dark-eyed doctor. Dr Schmidt, another neonatologist, petite and impeccable. The bleary woman, I realize, is the nurse who spent so many hours attending the baby. She was off yesterday — the news devastated her when she came on-shift this morning. My eyes settle on each face. I try to imagine who these people are. It occurs to me they may be making the same effort.

These caregivers have carved time out of the intense demands of the NICU to come to me, their faces drawn with grief and exhaustion. They gather around the bed, summoning strength, summoning breath. Summoning details about Chloe — the way she held her fists, the shape of her mouth, her tenacity. They speak, and then silence emerges from sound, swallows them into the ache of memory. They are struggling, these people: their skills and determination and imagination have been outmanoeuvred by death. Failure hunches their backs, makes awkward their idle hands.

I do not see failure. I am moved by their willingness to come to me, a woman who's been absent from the bedside of her baby, with stories of her baby's short life. I know, suddenly and certainly, that these people have loved, have *cherished*, our baby. It stuns me. Stumbling, I name their gifts: compassion, patience, fortitude, generosity, humour, grace. Together we begin to comprehend the absolute beauty of a life of days, release ourselves into mourning.

My mom arrives with the journal, and before they return to their work, each of these visitors writes a note. They speak their sorrow and sympathy, they speak of work and joy and courage. They have no answers. *In my country,* Dr Shah writes, *we believe that it's not the length of the life that matters, but the size. Your daughter's huge spirit moved us all.*

In minutes, they have gone, and hours from now, we will have left too. What remains: the feel of them, circled around my bed, a ring of grieving strangers, generous and bowed with loss. The baby's other family, foreign and familiar.

GETTING INTO THE CAR is far more challenging than I imagined. Even with my abdominal incision healing well, a week is scant recovery for muscles and tissues. The car seat is lower than the wheelchair, and you have to lift your legs to swing them inside — the task almost bests me. I get my body settled, and set about finding ease for the rest of me too. At least I feel safe here in the company of loved people, all three of us breathing air saturated with roses and lilies.

We have over an hour's drive to get from Hamilton to Waterloo. Every bump, every lurch, every adjustment in speed rattles up through my body. Still, it's amazing to be out — I feel like a small creature blinking in sudden light. The streets are fast and busy, then we break out into the stretch of fields, the periodic scatter of village storefronts. I watch these displays through the car window. I'm moving through an expansive movie set, the landscape of a dream. I am remote, disconnected from the lives humming along to unseen directives.

I feel like Eurydice, stripped of her reality, her dreams, her self, beginning the arduous trek out of the underworld. She cannot see, but she can hear — faintly — the compelling music of living and loving. Her task is to trust and to follow.

Bill and Mom and I drive through the late afternoon light. One week ago, we first laid eyes on our baby, our fiercely beautiful, fiercely alive Chloe. Now we watch lives flicker past the windows, each of us wondering how to navigate our own particular version of return. We steady the trembling flowers in the back seat. We speak now and then, and we listen to our own thoughts. Gradually, we make our way home.

We finally come to rest in the driveway, three aching people and a million blossoms. I struggle up steps with an armload of white lilies, shooting stars for the plain earth.

Wednesday, November 29, night

I LURCH UP THROUGH LAYERS OF TERROR, my eyes flying open in the dark. My own bed, the air of my own house. I am home, then. Yes, I came home today.

I lie still, trying to account for the racing heart. A dream, a nightmare — I was dying. I lie still a moment longer, separating dream self from waking one. I shift myself onto my side, arms compensating for a damaged torso.

Bill? I'm surprised by the strangle in my voice. *Bill — I think something's wrong.*

This patient, besieged man lunges upright, blinks himself conscious. *What is it?* he asks.

Now that I'm awake, I wonder if I have invented distress, dragged it up from the darkness. *I don't know,* I say. *I just — no, I don't feel right. I dreamed I was dying.*

After years of training nurses in anatomy labs, Bill can translate between inner and outer in a way that is beyond me. He straps his archaic blood pressure cuff around my upper arm, pumps the bulb with his thumb. The stethoscope cools a circle at my elbow. He checks, checks again, then clambers out of bed, pulls on his jeans and a sweatshirt. *We're going to the hospital,* he announces, helps me out of bed.

At 2 a.m. in the middle of the week, the hospital emergency ward is quiet. An old drunk hollers from his bed by the nursing station, and the nurses scold and tease in response. Mostly the city is hushed by sleep, and the nurses move efficiently in this half-empty place.

Bill gives the nurse a brief medical history, but the emergency doctor is busy in surgery at the moment, treating victims from a car accident. Every twenty minutes or so, the nurse stops by to take blood pressure readings, records them on the chart. Bill paces. He knows more than he should about potential health disasters — it worries him that my readings are steadily inching up. As I lie on this skinny bed, I know why I dreamed I was dying: my head is in a vice, my body is being tightened like a drum. Bill heads to the desk to ask when the doctor will come; the nurse doesn't know. He asks if there's another doctor on call; she puts him off. Finally, to appease him, she comes to check my readings again. The numbers climb.

Suddenly I have to pee. I can't even move, so the nurse brings a bedpan, leaves Bill to help me use it. Lifting my body is now a gruelling task — I am nailed to the bed by some relentless force. I'm beginning to feel afraid. Bill curls his arm behind my back, eases me partway toward sitting. I swing my knees up, perch awkwardly, and relieve my bladder, weeping with the effort. I sink down again, breathing under the unthinkable weight of my own blood.

Another half hour passes, and then another. We listen vaguely to the banter with the drunk. Finally Bill goes to the desk, demands to know when we will see a doctor. *My wife is seriously ill in there,* he sputters, *and if she's not going to get attention here, I'll take her back to Hamilton where the doctors know her situation.* The nurse blocks and parries. I listen from my curtained cubicle, unable to imagine travelling anywhere for help.

Then, as if he's been conjured, the doctor ducks in through the curtains, casual and friendly. *What seems to be the problem?* he says. Bill catalogues the details: severe pre-eclampsia, premature delivery, continuing hypertension, spinal headache, baby death. The doctor reels back just perceptibly, suddenly serious. He checks my pressure: 220 over 130, seizure zone. He whistles in dismay, hurries to the station to check my chart. We hear him speak sharply to the nurse: *Why hasn't that woman been treated? She could have a stroke!* Then he returns with a hit of drugs. I close my eyes, swim back down toward the dream of death.

Thursday, November 30

WHEN I WAKE, IT'S DAYTIME AGAIN. I'm in a new hospital room, alone. I sink into the silence. It's Thursday — I work it out in my mind. One week ago, I woke in a different hospital room. That was my first morning of motherhood. I think about that. Wasn't I that baby's mother before she faced the assault of air? When does a woman become a mother? It's a perplexing question, trickier than it seems. A week ago, I woke in a room that felt a universe away from my baby. This morning, my room is a universe away from my baby. Different. Same.

I am still sick, that much hasn't changed. The coordinated team of white coats takes away blood and urine samples, administers medications, charts my stubbornly resistant blood pressure. Usually the symptoms of pre-eclampsia subside with the delivery of the baby, but it's a complex disease — unpredictable and idiosyncratic, as well as challenging to study. These caregivers are now learning the way it manifests itself in my body, and they're watching for stress to my heart as well as my kidneys and liver. If this illness is poorly managed, it can leave a woman with permanent damage.

In the afternoon, I meet the nephrologist, a kidney specialist who is determined to tame my blood pressure. He's a tall man, slightly hesitant. He pulls a chair over to the side of my bed, crosses one long leg over the other, and says, *You're a young, healthy woman. We'll get you well again.*

I am flooded with relief — I haven't allowed myself to realize how much I needed this kind of reassurance. It's a challenge to maintain your courage, especially when nobody really understands the course of this disease. He takes a minute to look at my chart, then grumbles that I have been treated with crude drug formulations where more sophisticated ones have been available, and there's no way I should have been released from hospital without an established plan for follow-up care. I feel myself relaxing in his presence — this is a man who will speak what he knows.

I also think: here, I am a single body manifesting a challenging disease; in that other hospital, I was part of a tangled chaos of emergencies. I can concentrate better now, I can be more attentive to the work of healing.

He studies his notes again, then sits back into his chair and looks up at me. *We're trying to have a baby ourselves*, he confides into the sunshine that warms the air between us. *It's not such a straightforward wish. We'll get you healthy again, so if you decide to have another —*

Our eyes will lock around this freighted possibility, the thing I hardly dare contemplate. I begin to imagine that I will be well.

I DRIFT IN AND OUT OF WAKEFULNESS for the next couple of days. While the medical team tinkers with drugs and dosages, my mind hovers around who I am now: a woman alone in a hospital room, a woman contemplating devastation.

A few friends drop by with books, music, chocolate, but there's very little consolation we can offer one another, apart from acknowledging an ache that beggars words. What I see in them is helplessness and worry. It occurs to me they have come to reassure themselves that I haven't left them too. In a way, I *am* gone from them: I no longer feel compelled by the daylight world, with its structures and language and outcomes. I am elsewhere, journeying with the mourners.

I do realize that many things are happening away from here — both my father and father-in-law are travelling in from their faraway homes, Bill is assembling people to cover time-sensitive tasks at his workplace and mine, my mom is fielding calls from concerned friends and family. I realize but I'm not engaged by those things. I'm learning to float on my small life raft, and this anonymous hospital room gives me the privacy I crave.

Occasionally I hear the mewing of newborn infants, sometimes the spirited roar of angry babies, so I know I've been placed at the far end of the maternity wing. I am curiously neutral about this — it's unthinkable that none of these sounds would be my baby, but at the same time I'm relieved that I am included in this company of mothers. Navigating that hallway is harrowing for my family and friends, but not more harrowing than what they are already holding close to them. All of us are learning to comprehend the absence of an actual baby, a baby with beautiful limbs, an aureole of fine hair, ink-blue eyes, delicate skin. There's a relationship between the reality of her absence and the reality of her presence — I will spend years wondering how to comprehend it.

Friday, December 1

ON FRIDAY, I WAKE from my morning rest to see a woman pulling a chair toward the bed. I hitch up inside. Contact is taxing; I don't have the reserves to sustain much. She tells me she's the social worker assigned to this ward, and is dropping by to check on everybody. There's something about her breezy manner that puts me off. She might be the social convener up here on the maternity ward, but I'm not exactly a charter member, and anyway, this isn't really my hospital. I don't want to be one of her charges.

So, she says, leaning forward as instructed in her training manual. *So, you've had a big loss?* She nods expectantly, arranging her features to transmit concern.

Something huge shakes loose in me, a volcanic anger I've never encountered before. How dare she even speak to me? She knows nothing of what it means to be robbed of your own child, abandoned to an ache so enormous there are no words, no sounds, no gestures that can even begin to delineate it. How dare she intrude into my place of retreat and speak so casually, so stupidly, about something she cannot fathom? What makes her dream I would speak with her when the inside of me is so bruised, so tender, so vulnerable, that it can hardly bear exposure to the air?

I am desperate for her to be gone from me, but my words have been cauterized. I huddle under my blankets, look away. She pauses, then explains that lovely women from the area make baby quilts especially for women like me, women who don't end up taking home babies, and would I like one?

You're hurting me, says the strangled voice in my head.

No, I manage to say out loud. *No.* I close my eyes until I'm sure she is gone.

I AM STEADIED BY DROP-INS from Bill and Mom. When my dad arrives, I fall to pieces in his arms. He has mourned a baby's death too and knows this landscape with its bright shards of pain — I have no need to explain myself. It's both a terror and a relief to be so broken. For a few moments, I feel I might have wept myself clear.

But it's not clarity that eludes me: I see with terrible precision what is true. What I cannot see is how to live with it. I hover between my life and my loss, a static place, an in-held breath. I don't much want to talk, or even read — language belongs to others. I can hardly bear to be touched, except by people I cherish. I find some solace in music, and I begin to map my waking hours with Palestrina and Bach, austere, ethereal music, played so low I'm barely conscious of it. The lines weave through the chaos and reach me, like messages from another time, assertions of beauty, delicacy, intention. I feel accompanied.

I am not exactly lost, but where I am now is not familiar either. At the end of a hallway, I am mother and not-mother, shadowed by muted infant cries and the gradual onslaught of grief.

Saturday, December 2

BY SATURDAY NOON, the medical team is confident that my new regimen of medication is working, and I am released. I feel shaky and weak, but I am ready to be at home. I want to be with my husband and parents, I want to sleep in my own bed. I am ready.

Sunday, December 3

SINCE OUR RETURN TO WATERLOO on Wednesday, people have been calling with sympathy and concern, with tenderness, with offers of anything a body could need: nourishment, time, company, beauty. Bill and I realize we need to make an occasion for all of these people to find us, to find each other, to find our missing daughter. Bill posts notes in our university departments. He calls close friends with lists of people to contact. He invites people as they call. *Sunday afternoon, at our home, please come.*

On Sunday morning, Mom and I tidy the upstairs bedroom, bring up the miraculous bouquet of white lilies which continues to bloom. We set out the journal and a pen alongside a letter I have written, a brief version of a brief life. We lay out the tiny wristband — it fits my thumb precisely — and the tape measure torn raggedly at 13 ½ inches. We lay out the white dress Chloe wore at her death, the small knitted hat she wore at her birth. We set out her footprints, her handprints, the paper decorations from her isolette, the floppy-eared bunny. Small details, painfully intimate. I attend to these things, position and reposition them, try to find a shape, a context. I want, more than anything, to make these small things beautiful. They must be worthy.

It's context, really, that I long for, context so that I can comprehend where I am. In the wake of this birth, this death, I cannot understand what has happened, I cannot understand what it means. My arms ache with the lack of this daughter, and I cannot reach her with words or dreaming. I am filled with dread that the few precious threads I grasp so tightly will fade and be lost to me. I wonder what I will know as the days gather themselves into weeks, months, years. I wonder what I will lose and what I will find.

On this Sunday morning, all I can do is prepare myself for this day. I have written what I can about the short history of our travels. I have gathered and grouped the small things, then added the scent of lilies. I have slept to restore my ravaged body, then dressed myself in proper clothes. I have done these things because they are right, they are the rites.

I have done these things because they distract me from what is ahead: waves of sympathy, the awkward pain of friends and colleagues, the endless assault of proximity.

WHEN PEOPLE ARRIVE THAT AFTERNOON, the house smells of warm spices — cinnamon, cloves, allspice. Our parents meet people at the door, invite them in. *Take your coats upstairs to the bedroom,* they say. *And please take a moment to sign the journal with a note for Charlene and Bill. Yes, a few of Chloe's things are up there as well. Then come down for mulled cider...*

Hesitation, relief: anxious bodies arrive and find their welcome. Each one moves upstairs, grateful for privacy to cushion this meeting and farewell. I will read their notes, later, and they will break me open: people I know well and people I hardly know, all speaking simply, directly, gently, sadly. These persons, in the quiet of that space, have touched the small wristband, wondered at the hat, the tape measure, the tiny hands and feet. They thank us for introducing our daughter; some address her directly. They speak about hope and fear and sadness, they speak about dignity and courage. The notes are unnerving, profound. I will read them, off and on, for years. It will surprise me, each time, that this baby actually exists for these speakers, that in spite of her private, solitary life, she also has a public self, a self far exceeding my reach.

Our friends carry their ragged pain up the stairs, and come down calm, one after another. They find a cup of warm cider, speak with one another, then wind toward Bill, toward me. Fear cracks away, frees their grief-stricken selves to meet us here on this small island of warmth.

A colleague stoops toward me, shyly offers his sympathy. I urge my body upright, embrace him, embrace his wife. This is what we all need, over and over: the solid contact of living bodies, and forgiveness for our ridiculous failure to offer solace to one another. As I collapse into my seat, I realize I haven't accounted for a body only a dozen days from surgery. I don't have the strength to sit and stand, not repeatedly, yet I cannot forego this contact. I make my way across to the rocking chair by the room's entrance. I will be able to reach up and embrace from there, and people can crouch beside me to talk.

I learn later that one of my friends arrives, then flatly refuses to enter. After a bit, she comes into the warm house, braves the ghost of our gone baby, and the ghosts of children she mourns but will never bear. As the afternoon slows, she and her friends sit in a ring around my chair, and ask me to tell my whole story. For a suspended half-hour, their company will lift me into language, into narrative, into the miracle and terror of this event which threatens to capsize me. I feel their open hunger for this baby, their uncomplicated welcome of her tiny, secret self.

Our house fills to bursting with people. Something over a hundred friends — how can that be? The space crackles with energy, generosity, courage. We share words, and we step over into territory where words cannot follow. We approach and retreat, braving the intimacy of sorrow. We connect, simply and deeply. We are a community of grieving people, and we gather, supporting one another in an effort that feels too big for any one of us. My dad will say, tonight at supper, *These people all came for you, for Chloe.* He will shake his head, amazed.

It is demanding, this afternoon of contact, and before sharing a meal with the friends who stay to help clean up, I collapse into sleep. Shreds of laughter filter up into the bedroom, speckle my sleep with hope, with comfort. The lilies sing gently in the low light.

Tuesday, December 5

ON TUESDAY, I TAKE MYSELF to Christopher's design studio. I leaf through binders of paper, relieved by their exotic names, the polish of their surfaces. My mom is here, I'm glad of that. She is able to watch me fold up and unfold again. She seems to have confidence in me. By moments, I have it too.

I am here to invent an announcement of Chloe's death, a birth announcement that can do double-duty. Christopher, I know, will make it beautiful. He aches for me, he aches for Bill, he aches for our small daughter. He's a good man, this friend, and today's task requires of him a complex dance: approach the mourner, protect the mourner. He's gentle but sunny — that releases me into my task. I flip through binders of paper, and keep returning to parchment. There's something ethereal, fragile, lovely about parchment, yet some density too, echoes of scrolled announcements, biblical injunctions, meticulous record-keeping by solitary scribes in some other time and place.

I've brought the inkprints of Chloe's feet, perfect prints of perfect feet, unutterably small. They signal, better than anything, the extremity of this place I'm inhabiting. How could any feet be this tiny? Could the fierce, spirited baby, the baby who has died, have had feet this tiny? Perfect, human feet. How could I be a mother of a child with feet so tiny? How could the wearer of these feet be dead? How could I be the mother of a dead baby? I skitter toward the feet, I skitter away from them.

I try not to think about this part: the footprints were made after Chloe died. A nurse, gentle hands cradling this lost body, washed her, dressed her, photographed her. She printed her hands, printed her feet. She did these things, last rites, out of respect for this baby, and for her father who stood watch hour upon hour, for her damaged mother, for the grandmother who hovered between the baby and her own daughter.

I think of that nurse, there in the quiet room with my mom, each of them mourning the dead infant. I imagine them engaging in gentle talk, practical woman-talk, buttoning small buttons, coaxing cool feet onto an ink pad. Both of them will have marveled at the sturdiness of a body so small, and the quiet finality of death. My mom, surely, held my baby and thought of her own gone baby, of all that she hadn't been allowed to do or feel or say all those years ago, the great weight of silence around infant death. My mom, finally allowed to visit old bruises, to offer herself and these small beings the grace of attention, the human longing for dignity, respect.

I hold the inkprints of Chloe's feet, and I keep returning to the pink parchment. I resolutely refused pink myself as a child — I was too proud for pink, too sensitive to the unstated equation of femininity and weakness. But now I know something else: a premature baby has so little fat that the narrow arms and feet, the round belly, the ears and fingers and neck and ankles are ruddy, the deepest pink. The blood that streams furiously around the tiny body is scarcely below the surface, boiling with resolve, on an imperious mission to feed, defend, rescue. How could I choose green, or beige, or burgundy? Pink is a softer-than-Chloe colour, but it's her colour. She spent her days naked, wearing her skin bravely and with determination. I know now that pink is a tough colour.

Christopher hovers, solicitous, anxious to put his skills to use. He scans the footprints into his computer, clucks over their perfection, then busies himself in the next room. I sit next to my mom and reel into fathomless sorrow. How can I announce the death of our daughter? Are there words for death?

I can't do this, I weep, *I can't do this*.

The pen in my hand writes Chloe's name, her birth date, her weight. The pen stops, I struggle for air. The pen writes, *She was a surprised parcel* — yes, that's exactly it. The muscles of my face contort. The pen writes, *She earned her wings in the quiet of the afternoon.* The pen marks and marks, scratches meaning onto a scrap of paper. I hunch over the pen in breath-holding agony.

Christopher returns, gently takes the scratches and enters them into his computer. He moves the perfect feet around, a bodiless dance, finally sets them at the bottom of the page. The text bends and curves, makes a life-path of six days.

We will send this beautiful note with its bravely dancing feet, this missive of birth and death. Readers across the country will open it, their hands quivering slightly as they hold this parchment with its words that spell a life. They will glimpse the promise of death for each of us, and the possibility of beauty.

I FALL ASLEEP THAT NIGHT AND DREAM OF UNCLE BOB. Even in my dream, I know he is dead — we reach toward one another across the border that separates the living from the no longer living.

The two of us talk lightly, lovingly. He has come to tell me something, but first he asks, *How is it for you?* In the way of dreams, I tell and tell — *I have lost my baby, I am in anguish, I cannot breathe, I have lost my baby.* The words float free of me, uninflected. I tell because this man knows. He has mourned, he has been mourned. Even as I weep out my heartbreak, I pay attention. This is an audience, I will miss none of it.

When the dream is ending, I am buoyed toward consciousness by his voice. *All things will be well,* he says, *all manner of things will be well.* The phrase circles and circles, a litany to move me into another day. I blink into the early light, calm and determined. I will hollow out a space for this gone child, this fiery spirited daughter. She will dance as far as my memory can reach.

I am certain that my uncle's muscled arms are sweeping her into the air in the way I remember so clearly. She shrieks with joy, learning the glory of falling and flight.

WINTER WEATHER

December 1995 – March 1996

although winter may be everywhere
with such a silence and such a darkness
— e.e. cummings

I stand at the doorway to my kitchen and right before my eyes, the season changes. Gusts of winter blow across the window. Sudden ice, bitter wind. I must get the baby, I think. Desperation lurches up, tightens my throat. I left the baby on the front porch — I must get the baby! I'm stricken, immobilized with dread. Then I remember: there is no baby. I have put a baby carriage on the porch to fool myself. I have no baby. I'm the woman who is destined to push an empty carriage through the streets, muttering and weeping. People will look away.

Monday, December 11, 1995

IT'S A CHALLENGE TO RE-ENTER YOUR LIFE when the scripts have been dramatically altered. Bill and I spend a couple of days drifting through the rooms of our home. We watch one another, wonder what triggers are waiting in ambush, what consolation might rest in familiar objects or rituals.

We are together in grief, we are separate in grief. This is our new land.

I am desperately tired. Surgery and on-going hypertension have taxed my system, but sorrow — sorrow is a mountain I am climbing every waking minute. For the first time in my life, I am not a robust, healthy woman. It occurs to me I am being offered a lesson in humility. I am an unwilling student.

We had planned to spend the holidays in Waterloo, preparing our home to welcome a baby. Bill is keen to stay that course. He is ready to reclaim some solitude, then gather his scattered resources toward winter courses which start in only three weeks. I hardly feel strong enough to care for myself, let alone cope with a home that aches for a child. I want to retreat into the arms of my family; I want to be someone's child myself.

We talk a long time, finally arrive at a compromise. We will spend Christmas at my parents' home in Manitoba, he will fly back to Waterloo before New Year's to prepare his classes, and I will follow him back a couple of weeks later. It's a plan that can sustain us both. In the meantime, we have myriad tasks to attend to — groceries, letters, medical appointments, work obligations. I care about none of them.

Thursday, December 14, 1995

ON THURSDAY AFTERNOON, Bill and I come in from an errand, December bluster circling around our heels. I'm rarely out, it's both bracing and bewildering. I stamp the snow from my boots, gingerly shrug off my coat. I'm often caught off-guard by my post-surgery body — I have to be aware of how I move.

I've found an envelope tucked between the doors, a note from Betsy. I run my finger under the flap, open it up. Her handwriting, like her speech, is clear, direct. She's written to let us know there's a light on the city's memorial tree this Christmas in Chloe's memory.

I've looked forward to watching your little one play in the park, the note says. *I thought she needed to have a light there. At the least.*

My throat squeezes shut and I'm struck again at the peculiar twinning of anguish and swallowing. Perhaps feeling chokes us, or perhaps the body is determined to announce what it resists. *Of course, Betsy,* I whisper to the page in my hand. *Thank you...*

Every gesture which places my gone daughter into the world strikes me dumb with fear. These spider filaments feel dangerous. They are unlawful, I will be punished. Yet each day is rife with them: might haves and could haves, elusive futures.

As I hold Betsy's note, I am suddenly imagining a little girl, my little girl, squealing skyward on the swings, or dancing through the flowering labyrinth. I think of her clambering up Betsy's front steps to ask for a glass of water. She hopes she might be invited in for a cookie, a conversation, a quiet moment in a rocking chair with an old stuffed bear who's lost one eye. The specificity of what can't happen is disorienting. Devastation is in the detail.

Still, a light on a tree is a kind of presence. *A child lived*, it says, in its wordless way, *a child was loved.*

Or, more truly: *Someone loves this child.*

Later that afternoon, Bill comes back from a snowy walk and announces that he has located the memorial tree, a strapping young spruce just half a block past Betsy's rambling home. It's shining with lights, and alive with the flutter of small white cards, each tied with a length of white ribbon. *I opened each card*, he says, *until I found Chloe's name.*

We are silenced by that thought. Then we hold one another, and weep for the promise of her there, apart from us, bigger, in the world.

Saturday, December 16, 1995

AT OUR CHLOE GATHERING, Ted and Donna gave me a small satin pillow their daughter Haley made for me: uneven stitches, looping thread, a gift of feeling. Haley, freshly ten, is a girl with spirit — she stole my heart when we first moved here three years ago. Despite our difference in age, we are friends.

I call Haley. We arrange that I'll come for lunch, and then she and I will share tea and talk. When I arrive, she wraps her arms around me. Her worry and sorrow swamp us, and then pass. I sit with this loved family at their table, and the talk is light and gentle. As the meal ends, our backs stiffen with shyness. *Maybe you and Haley would like tea in the other room*, Donna says.

A girl and a woman sit side by side in the parlour of a grand old house, and contemplate the aching void of sorrow. I hesitate, as I do each time. How can I speak to a child of the vulnerability we all share? Will I die of sorrow in the telling?

Are you afraid? I ask. She nods.

We steel ourselves, then I set out my treasures. The tiny wristband, the paper tape measure, the doll-sized hat. It's hard to fathom a baby so small. She listens and wonders. *Did you bury her?* she asks. *Were you with her when she died?* Occasionally we weep. I am struck, as always, by her fortitude.

Her brother sidles into the room, eyes carefully avoiding mine. He plays near the couch, then plants his head into the cushions. He's here and not here, face hidden but ears unprotected. He wants to know, but six-year-old intuition is well-tuned for survival. He dances with dread, turns his back on me to protect himself. Haley frowns at him, looks back at me knowingly.

This powerful girl and I sit together a few minutes longer, and then we're finished. We blink, breathe deeply, drag sunlight into our shared spaces. I am clearer than when I arrived, less afraid of myself. We hold one another for a long moment, then she travels back to her childhood. I travel forward, blessed by her bravery.

December 18 – 22, 1995

THE DAYS PILE UP. I slip birth announcements into envelopes along with the letter I've written for our Chloe gathering. I take calls from people far away. Whenever I can, I hide out in my room and rest.

My mom fills the kitchen with the smell of Christmas baking and we deliver boxes of sweet things to our friends. We even drive down to Hamilton and leave baking for the nurses and doctors on the wards. Mom and I drive across to London — she is searching for snowshoes to surprise Dad at Christmas.

I enter into these things as best I can, but I have limited energy, and even less interest. Inertia is my new familiar. I am beyond initiating anything, and I have difficulty sustaining my engagement in even small tasks. I will follow for a bit, but then I just veer off and collapse. I am heavy company — I feel how my sadness and fatigue burden those around me, and it wears me out to reassure them. I am staggering under my own weight. I am busy.

Finally, we throw a few essentials into a suitcase and fly back to Manitoba. I am hollow and grey.

Christmas, 1995

CHRISTMAS IS NOT EASY. The traditions, the carols, the narrative of nativity — the whole season is an assault on my exposed nerve endings. I feel fragile.

The day before Christmas, my sister and her husband drive out to Boissevain from Winnipeg. My brother and his wife arrive with their three-year-old daughter. Eight sombre adults, one precocious child. We gather together because that is what we are able to do. We recognize the tear in the fabric of our family, but we don't focus on it. There's nothing much to be done apart from sharing this time. Mending is slow work.

The Christmas Eve service is an agony for me. I cannot bear these carols, these readings. I don't want to be in my childhood church with all these adults who've watched me grow. It's painful to feel the concern of my family, all of us helpless to ease this distress. I retreat into myself, a weeping, ragged mess.

On Christmas morning, little Emily dispenses hugs and kisses, and does her best to leaven the mood. She is eager to give us her present. She and her mom have made Christmas tree decorations from playdough: tiny feet and tiny hearts, painted with a child's passion for colour, and topped off with a flourish of sparkles. They are spectacular. I wrap my arms around her, and she's delighted. When my eyes well up, she asks her mama, *Why is Auntie so sad? Is it because of Baby Chloe?* I fear my heart will shatter.

My sister, always reserved in the face of oversized emotion, has found her own way to speak. As the last of the wrapping paper is cleared away, she hands me a small package. I see, as I open it, that she has spent the last month searching: I hold in my hands a perfect angel.

Wednesday, December 27, 1995

WE HAVE CARRIED OUR CHLOE TREASURES to Manitoba, and before Bill returns to Waterloo, we invite our family and friends to join us at my parents' home. Mom and Dad know first-hand how important it is to create a reality here for this baby, and to make an opportunity for family and friends to attend to us all.

We lay out the journal and markers of Chloe's life in the bedroom at the end of the hall. I spend much of my afternoon there, talking quietly with people in ones or twos, telling my stories to people who've been part of my life since childhood. I feel less raw than I was when people gathered at our Waterloo home, but I feel more separate from myself too, as if conversation is a trick I can do.

Still, there is solace — for me, for Bill, for my parents, as well as for these people who come to mark the birth of our baby. My father's sister holds Chloe's tiny hat in her hand, then shares her private recollections of my parents' baby who died more than forty years ago, her anguish at that loss, her remorse at not marking and mourning that death and life more fully. As I listen, it dawns on me that a life might be ephemeral — viewed from a distance, every life is ephemeral — but a life might also be tough and lasting.

Perhaps our baby, too, will generate stories in forty years. Perhaps our baby, too, will continue to matter.

Thursday, December 28, 1995

BILL RETURNS TO WATERLOO and the demands of teaching and research. I feel the terrible weariness in him, but I also feel his growing need for structure, goals, clarity. He needs his students, his projects, his deadlines. They are demanding, but they will steady and strengthen him.

For me, that world of work makes me quake. My impulse now is to flee from structures. I understand the therapeutic value of work, but I know from experience that grieving is a kind of work too. After my miscarriage, I pushed aside the inner demands in deference to the demands of my classrooms. By the time my school term ended, I was anxious, resentful, and exhausted from resisting the clamour inside. I will not make that error again.

Friday, December 29, 1995

WHEN THE CIRCLE SHRINKS back to just my parents and me, I feel sad but calm. They make room for me, but they don't call on me. I can stretch out and listen to music or linger over a jigsaw puzzle. I can rest myself, body and spirit.

One afternoon, we drive out to a farm where my parents' friend Tom has offered to take us out in his horse and cutter. We bring my dad's two sisters. They reminisce about taking a cutter to school, one time tipping out the teacher who boarded in their crowded farmhouse. Accidentally, of course. We bundle into warm coats and wait along the lane. Their excitement is infectious.

When Tom brings the cutter up from the barn, my lively aunts are suddenly bashful. They wonder if they remember how to clamber into a cutter, they wonder what it might mean to ride in one at a distance of so many decades. Tom grins, a sparkly-eyed boy inside a moustached man. The women settle into the seat beside him.

When they come back up the lane twenty minutes later, their delight slices through the frozen air. They are aging widows suddenly offered their youth. Aunt Alice throws her head back and swallows the early dusk. She can't remember when she has been this happy.

I stand still in the snow, an eager witness. I watch their faces crack open in the radiance of what is gone. Then I am careening toward the roaring silence which partners me every minute. I grasp for the thing I see in those faces, whatever it is that imbues precious losses.

Tom helps the women out, waits quietly for me. I am almost too freighted to move. My dull limbs climb in, and Tom calls to the horse. It paces down the snowy lane. Gradually, the sway of the cutter and the quiet ease of this man loosen me, and I am released into the late-day sky, first scatter of stars. *I have lost my baby, I have lost my baby*: chant of hooves, song of snow.

We ride in silence, half-buried barbed wire fences marking our progress toward no goal. I could ride all night. At some point, we turn around, head back to light and people and the effort of contact. Tom clears his throat, glances sideways to hold my eyes. *Don't worry about your mom and dad*, he says. *We'll be near, we'll let them speak.*

I nod. A piece of me shifts into a new position, relaxes in this frozen, open space. *Do you have someone to talk to at home?* he asks. He is gentle, respectful. *You need to have people who will listen — we all need that.*

The cutter turns into the lane. I understand that I am turning toward something, heart broken open and ready.

Sunday, December 31, 1995

TWO NIGHTS LATER, we are making another drive back to town from Tom's farm, this time sated with a New Year's Eve feast. I've made it to the gate of a new year, which feels like cause for celebration. The engine drones, the car murmurs over the gravel road. I'm wrapped in the dark of my childhood, private and secure. I could be ten again, riding home from Grandma's house, faking sleep in the driveway so that I will be carried in by strong arms.

Earlier today, I spoke with Bill in Waterloo. Our friends have invited him to share the evening with them — I am glad he will be accompanied into a new year too. We talked a long time on the phone, warming the intervening distance with the minutiae of our days. Before we hung up, we recognized the demands of where we are, then offered our winnowed selves into the safekeeping of the year ahead.

In the back seat of my parents' car, I can't see the year ahead — I can't see past this minute. I stretch, shift positions, wish I'd eaten less turkey. By the time we arrive home, I have a champion gut ache. I chew down antacid tablets, wrap a towel around a hot water bottle, lean over the puzzle pieces at the big table. My parents think about sleep, then choose to join me instead. It's two in the morning, the world hushed, suspended like ice crystals in prairie air. Except for the pain in my belly, I am at peace. I groan, sigh, shift on my chair.

I remember, my dad begins, *when I was a kid, sometimes the cows would get The Bloat.* I hear the capitals, grin to myself. I've always loved my dad's stories, their economy, their shrewd translation of particulars. I have no idea what The Bloat is; I'm a town kid, and a different generation. My mom nods, smiling at the piece in her hand. *If cows get into something they shouldn't — alfalfa, or grain spilling out of a granary — they get terrible gas, it just swells them up, their bellies hard as rocks.* I think about this, press the water bottle onto my own distended belly. This is good, this is what I need.

Yeah, it'll kill 'em, The Bloat, says my dad. *That stuff ferments in there.* In the inner monologue that parallels the story, I pause: *it'll kill 'em.* I stretch, try to breathe down into the pain. *You had to let that gas out, before it killed 'em. We used to pierce right through the hide. A knitting needle'd do it, just poke through, let the gas out.* He places a piece into the sky.

I laugh out loud, then shudder. How much force would you need to poke a hole in cowhide? What kind of desperation? *Got any knitting needles around here, Mom?* I ask. *I could really use one.* I stretch my back to make enough room for the ache, settle into the puzzle.

I'm aware of being the child of these two amazing people. I'm aware of the calm spaces they create for me here in the nest of my childhood, and of their own younger selves, the decades-old and newly fresh grief of infant death that shapes their days as well as mine. I am aware of the adult I have become in their presence, of the new configuration of family we're learning to realize. They are grandparents to my child, a child my father has never seen. I imagine they have spoken together about her, about me, about the aching ordeal of loss and survival. They let me speak — they will always let me speak — but they don't seem to need me to speak. They hold enough in their hands to make sense of where I am. They reach out, leave me room to move toward and away.

I take a fresh hot water bottle to bed, fidget my way toward sleep. I doze, then wake. I get up, head to the bathroom, return to bed. I'm gasping, sweating, struggling. Mom materializes, summoned by sharp hearing or intuition, and wonders if we need to head to the hospital. I hesitate, heave myself out of bed, decide, *Yes, yes, I need help.*

New Year's Eve, halfway to dawn, and I'm in the emergency room of a small-town hospital. Nurses bustle around, call the doctor to come. Many of them know the shell of my story already, and they're anxious to bring what ease they can. I am nearly blind with the pain. A belt cinches around my ribs, robs me of breath and voice. I hunch up on all fours, grimacing. The belt tightens. I'm a cat, or a bloated cow.

Or a woman in labour. I suddenly see it, am stiff with embarrassment. How could I have come here, crippled by a dream of labour? I can hardly bear myself.

The doctor arrives, burly and affable, asks me to describe what's happening. I choke out bits of information and he digs his fingers under my rib cage, searches behind his eyelids for insight. A shot of Demerol, a dose of muscle relaxant, and the symptoms gradually ease. Acute indigestion, that's what he supposes. And grief, though he doesn't say that out loud. He returns to his sleep, I curl toward my mom.

Before they can move me to a room, I am overtaken by another bout. My face contorts. Mom catches my eye, laughs, then sobers. *I thought you were just making a face*, she says. *That would be like you, to make a face —*

My belly shudders, taut, beleaguered. *I am trying to have a baby*, I think, *I am trying to have a baby*. It humiliates me to witness this misguided will, my body's determination.

I lower myself into a hot bath — I want to avoid another dose of Demerol as long as I'm able. I don't like the thickness that blankets down on me, the disorientation, the anxiety. I add and add and add hot water, struggle toward the dawn and a new year.

January 1996

I AM RELEASED FROM HOSPITAL two days later, exhausted and sore. A few hours later, my mom whisks me back in the midst of another attack, and the nurse pumps in a shot of Demerol before calling for an appointment with the specialist. She makes a friendly bet with the doctor that I have gallstones. In a couple of days, the specialist in Brandon confirms her suspicion: my gallbladder is full of gravel. The nurse and doctor assemble in my room to deliver the news. She collects her ten-dollar bill, laughing good-naturedly.

I find out later that almost one in ten women develop gallstones in pregnancy — apparently this is one of those design problems that evolution hasn't yet resolved. Pregnancy hormones and slower digestion can make the gallbladder less efficient, and when crystals begin to develop, they clog up the process even more. They also hurt — think of squeezing a handful of sharp stones day after day. If one gets pushed into the bile duct, the pain is excruciating. *Like labour*, some women say, *except without pauses.*

I'm not happy to have gallstones, but I am relieved. At least I know what I'm dealing with, and if I am scrupulous about avoiding all fat and being cautious about fibre-dense foods, I should be able to sidestep another attack. All of us hope that I can be transferred from this hospital to the hospital in Brandon, an hour away, to have the offending organ removed right away, but schedules everywhere are over-crowded. Bill enlists the help of our family doctor in Waterloo, and I'm booked in for early February. It's a long time to make do on unbuttered bread and well-cooked vegetables and clear tea. I can see that I may have to become an expert soup maker.

WITH FOOD OFF THE LIST of things we can share together, my parents offer the prairie. We drive aimlessly, following the gravel roads which cut the flat land into square miles. I have always been mesmerized by the long march of fence posts, the hydro poles with their swooping lines. Now that I live far away, I marvel at how uncrowded it is out here — off the main highways, we drive for hours and meet only the occasional farm truck. Space around buildings, space around people, and all of us small under the dome of sky.

There is plenty of snow this year. The winds that clip across the open miles have created meandering sculptures in the ditches, and the snow shines blue in the afternoon light. Dad spots a snowy owl on a fence post half a mile ahead of us. We slow down so we won't startle it as we approach. It is a huge bird, majestic. It waits for us to arrive, then lifts its enormous wings and drifts ahead, settling on another post. We follow it for miles in this frozen landscape. I am far from happy, but I discover I am still capable of awe.

We drive out into the country most days. We have no destination — we are simply moving together through spaces we love, spaces which ask nothing of us. I'm alone in the back seat with my thoughts and the lull of movement. I listen to the weaving of my parents' voices, a duet refined over many years. I listen to the way they share silence too. Sometimes I sit forward and add my words to theirs, mostly I settle back on this cushion of privacy and calm.

The car with its three passengers is a determined little satellite, orbiting a vanishing star. When I seize up with anguish, my mom reaches back and lays her hand on my knee. Sometimes I think I will die from a broken heart. Sometimes I wish I could.

THE DAY BEFORE I RETURN to Waterloo, we wake up to silvery trees, so we head south from town, up into the bush. Tough, narrow aspen and birch, dogwood, hawthorn — every branch is a startle of hoarfrost against the cerulean sky. When I was a child, my mother would sing us out of sleep on a day like today. *It's fairyland,* she'd call, and we'd lunge toward the window to check for ourselves. The brilliance is something beyond beauty, something beyond astonishment: it compels me to hold it in my eyes. Branch upon branch, the scrubby bush is furred with crystals. It's cold, it's clear, it's ravishing.

A flock of sparrows — dull brown, nondescript — suddenly materializes above the treetops, stark against the blue. In a ribbon of movement, they traipse haphazardly after an accidental leader, resettle in another tree. *Who begins?* I wonder. *Who knows who to follow?* I watch them lift and settle, lift and settle. They flurry across the highway behind us. I watch the shape they create together, an undulation, a thing — both whole and inadvertent — that could, at any second, disintegrate into its separate, insignificant particles.

This cluster of birds, these blinding branches: I am being offered something. A lesson, of sorts, about accidental beauty, about the human wish to see meaning in every performance. About the mystery of ephemera, these small birds acting in concert. About the safety of childhood. About my own history of mourning. I see the possibility of my daughter, released from me.

I weep while the birds lift and settle. Far above, a white line appears in silence, a jet unzippering the blue sky on its way somewhere else.

I pull the car over to the side of the road. A wide ditch, then thick forest — this is a place I know, but more remote than I expect. The car is old and battered. I climb out, stand a moment looking down the stretch of asphalt. Silence. Stillness. I walk to the back of the car, open the trunk. A grand white bird, egret or swan, flaps into the air. Splayed wing, awkward flight. It leaves a trail of pain and recrimination. I look back at the captive passenger in the trunk of my car. A small mottled owl huddles on a burlap sack. It occurs to me that I have run into both birds in my rush to reach a place I cannot recall. I have damaged them: I am responsible. Complicity changes everything. The owl looks at me. It is small, surprised. Its muteness reproaches me.

I RETURN TO OUR HOME in Waterloo and take on the challenge of solitude. Each day Bill leaves for work and I make my way through the hours. I empty the mailbox, read cards and letters from faraway friends, hear their struggle with distance, disbelief, dismay. I sit next to myself, watch the relentless desire for comfort shudder through my bones. The cards and letters warm me, but they don't reach to the middle of me. The heart — a hawk, an eddy — spins and spins around its absent wish.

Time is suspended when you're mourning. Hours move past, but moments hang, swollen drops at the kitchen tap. I listen to music, I listen to silence. I cannot read a novel — I simply cannot follow a plot, and I don't trust it anyway. I can stand in the shower, at home in a pounding drama that has no point, no direction. I move from room to room. New baskets of plants dry out, wait patiently for attention. I plan to water them and forget. Their parched voices call.

The light leaves one room and wanders into the next, the grieving mother migrates with it. Time is vertical: there is no story here, no narrative to press a body from one moment into the next. A cup of tea, a pile of letters, a dream of comfort. I move up and down in my own body, navigating a deep pit of sorrow. I weep, often without warning, then, just as suddenly, I find myself lifted into something approaching relief.

In the first weeks of sorrow, there isn't much to be done. You remember, you forget. The wish that animates your days is also a wish you may never again hold. Its eyes are closed to you, its ears deaf to your calling. Sometimes the anguish of that will cripple you, sometimes you will shake it aside and glimpse something entirely neutral, something prior. Always, though, the longed-for is at the centre: it tethers you to it, a solid absence, a hole, a gash, a rent. A scandal. You would do anything — or, truthfully, anything but *this*, this endless, vertiginous circling. Suspension. Torpor.

The inside of a cocoon is dove-grey, soft as ash. Away from the crush of the world, a body hovers, inactive but not inert. Another life, a life after confinement: anything is possible.

I HADN'T BEEN ABLE TO OPEN THE CARDBOARD BOX with Chloe's ashes when Bill brought it home from the funeral chapel early in December. I was surprised by its plainness, though I shouldn't have been. What else to hold the remnants of a body's struggle toward breath and the world's demands? What else to hold a shattered heart? I couldn't bear to have the box sitting out, yet hiding it on the closet shelf seemed an indignity.

When I return to Waterloo, I bring with me a small raku pot, square and lidded, iridescent blue like the inner reaches of a flame. My sister built it, glazed it, fired it. I asked for it because it carries the traces of her hands. I wanted it because it tells its own stories of being baked brittle by fire, of being tempered and strengthened and made beautiful. I offer Bill its rugged beauty against the blandness of cardboard.

I come upon him one afternoon, spent with tears, crouching over it. He has transferred the tiny bag with its ash and bits of bone. He had made a home for his floating daughter. He hoped it was okay: he's tucked in petals from the lilies and roses, and a small wooden angel from our Christmas tree.

I am relieved. I am thankful.

It is several days before I can brave my terror, see with my own eyes the physical evidence of a tiny body. I lift the lid. What's inside is both unspeakable and commonplace, the traces of a life.

We set the box on the piano. The fired clay, the packet of ash, the desiccated petals, the wooden angel: they speak to one another, offer their voices to a story that outstrips speech.

I stand in the middle of what was once a house. The floor buckles and pitches away drunkenly. The walls lean like splintered bones. The roof is gone. I survey the wreckage, knowing this is my house. I shake my head

---

and sigh. Such a big task to heave all these broken parts into place. I am already weary.

THE WINTER DAYS ASSUME A RHYTHM. Bill pours his daytime energy into pursuing data and inspiring young students, then comes home to spend some quiet time with me before disappearing into his study to prepare the next day's classes.

I make bread almost every day. The process becomes my ritual, an assertion that I still belong in the company of women. Flour, water, yeast: with attention, simple things become complex, subtle, specific.

Each day, I press and press the heels of my hands into the bread, surrendering myself to the rhythm of the work. I am calling to the deep thing in me that has been so shaken. *I can nourish*, I am telling myself, *I can sustain.*

The voice behind that one knows something else. *You did not nourish*, it says. *You did not sustain. A mother is a safe house. You have failed.*

Still, the bread rises, day after day. The smell of it baking fills our home.

THE NOTE RESTING IN MY MAILBOX is from my father's older sister, a woman I have loved deeply since I was a child. I imagine her sitting at her kitchen table back in Manitoba, the winter sun filtering through the curtains and pooling around the velvet blooms of her violets. She's drinking a cup of hot tea, listening to the clock marking off the minutes in her quiet house. She picks up her pen and writes me her sadness, her concern, her care. She sips her tea, looks across the snowy back garden. She is thinking about the tulips that are hiding there, the rhubarb and asparagus. *Some gifts are hard to receive*, she writes.

A province away and a week later, I stand in my own frozen landscape and consider that thought. Chloe's death, Chloe's life: this pain might be a gift, if I can figure out how to receive it. That thought takes root in me like a stubborn prairie perennial. I too might be a garden when the weather changes.

JANUARY SUN IS FADED, FRAGILE like the inside of a petal. It floats through the window of my kitchen, finds me on my knees in a bare room. The table and chairs have been carted out in preparation for painting. We've finished the walls in a colour with the overtones of early dawn. I'm ready now for the wainscotting. I'm throwing caution to the wind, which is something I do rarely these days: I've bought a pail of brilliant pink.

I begin to stroke, a startling blaze of colour. I'm delighted. I dip and paint, dip and paint. The repetition relaxes me. I'm at ease here in the thin January light, putting summer lipstick on my walls.

By the time I finish the first wall, I'm weary. I wrap the brush, replace the paint lid, stretch. An hour on the couch and I've dozed my way to clarity again. I check the mail, get myself a drink of water at the bathroom sink. By the time I arrive at the kitchen door, I'm walking through a viscous soup of anxiety. Now I see that it's an impossible colour, a stupid decision, a mess. I stand, helpless, surveying the clutter of newspapers in a kitchen which has lost its light. The wainscotting, half-finished, is brazen and blotchy. I unwrap the brush, wrap it back up again. What am I doing?

Later I will realize that even simple tasks require more of a mourner. We mourners are more easily distracted, less courageous about our decisions. We struggle to access our energy reserves. Painting even a few feet of wainscotting might be considered an accomplishment, and selecting a brazen pink takes nerve. Today, though, cement pooling in my legs, anxiety choking the breath out of me, I'm not pleased, not proud. The brush hovers in my hand, I frown at myself, irritated. *I will do this thing,* I tell myself. I pry the lid from the pail, and I paint.

When Bill arrives in the last drops of daylight, I'm weeping in exhaustion and dismay. I can't stand it and I can't stop.

I like it! he says, grinning.

I know he is lying, salvaging the remnants of me from the bottom of the paint pail. I appreciate it.

No, I really do. Let it dry, love. If you don't like it, we can always paint over it.

I settle back on my heels and look at him across the litter of paint-specked newspaper. Just like that: we can reverse a decision, change the predicate. Only death is like death, I suppose. I have spent many hours imagining other outcomes than death, and the dreaming moves me nowhere, except closer to despair. There's no escape for a battered heart.

But paint? We can choose something else. If we want. We can choose.

My damaged body continues to do its work. My follow-up visit with the nephrologist is uncomplicated. He is pleased with my progress, and can see no indication that the hypertension has left permanent damage. We will continue the regimen of medication, and begin to wean off late in the spring. I trust him. It settles me that he is willing to follow me through this process.

I meet the surgeon who will remove my gallbladder. Surgery has changed since my dad was carved open for gallbladder surgery twenty years ago. Now they can inflate the abdomen and slide the surgical instruments inside the cavity. I will have small incisions, and a much quicker recovery. The surgeon details the process — he's done it a million times. There's an edge in his manner that appeals to me. He's smart and witty. He likes to be in charge.

When I visit my family doctor, we talk about the heavy effort of grief: the exhaustion, the anxiety, the blinding sadness. She reminds me that human experience has sweeping contours, and I will not be stranded here. She believes I will find my way. I tell her I'm beginning to be troubled by my right hip — it won't swivel the way I expect it to. When I get to the landing on the stairs, I have to turn my whole body to get around the corner. Also, my diaphragm is going into spasms without warning, leaving me bent over in pain, unable to move. I've been walking a block or two, but often my whole body will seize up completely and I'll be left standing on the sidewalk, gasping for breath. She reminds me that the ligaments around my hip joint are tightening up again in the aftermath of a pregnancy, and she suspects the diaphragm spasms are aftershocks from the gallbladder attack. *Keep working*, she says. *The whole body is one complex system. All of you is in recovery.*

Bill and I go together to Dr Halmo's office. I've sat in this waiting room often, squeezed in with all the expectant mothers, crossing and uncrossing ankles, flipping through aging magazines. Today we are not mothers in waiting, but other mothers: mothers who have failed to conceive, mothers who have failed to carry, mothers who have failed to bring their babies, safe, into an expectant home. We enter and exit efficiently because we are scheduled, tactfully, on particular days of the week devoted to the empty-bellied. We cross and uncross our ankles too, but we rarely leaf through the magazines. We can detail our deficiencies without the aid of blooming pregnant bodies in this season's business wear, or tips for post-natal exercise regimes. Radiant women, radiant babies. They are a long way from us.

When the doctor comes into the examining room, he brings his sympathy and concern along with his skills. He is a compassionate man. I feel more solid in his presence. He completes the six-week post-natal check-up, says he's pleased with my recovery. Apart from the slower-than-normal downward drift of the blood pressure, I'm healing well. Before we leave, he cautions us to wait several months before thinking about having another baby — I will need that much time to arrive at full health. He hesitates a moment. *Many people have a strong negative feeling about their doctor after a trauma like yours,* he says. *If you decide to become pregnant again and would rather see a different doctor, I will understand.*

Later, over tea, I share my relief and Bill counters with distress. As we talk, I realize he is certain the doctor has cautioned us not to have another child. I am certain he has encouraged us to try again. Neither of us has the nerve to ask him which is true.

February 1996

AFTER A MONTH OF CLEAR SOUP and unbuttered bread, I am glad enough to be getting rid of my gallbladder. I lie on another gurney in yet another hospital, preparing for the surgeon to poke holes in my belly. I think of my dad and the cows suffering The Bloat. I think of knitting needles puncturing tough hide. I think of being able to eat again. I think of being strong and well.

It doesn't escape me that I am losing this small, useless organ on the date we expected Chloe, but I won't speak of it for fear of hurting myself. The mask rests over my nose and I begin the countdown.

Laparoscopic surgery is much less challenging than the Caesarean section. In the aftermath, I am tender but not incapacitated. I have a small cut up near my sternum, another along my navel, and two puncture holes about three inches on either side of that midline. I feel good, better than I had expected. I feel relieved. I have to support my abdomen with a pillow, but I'm able to leave the hospital the next day and recuperate at home.

A week goes by, and another, and I feel strong enough to answer a summons that's been sitting just below my consciousness for weeks. I want to return to the hospital in Hamilton — I want to see Helen.

I step off the elevator onto the fourth floor. I head down the hall until I'm almost in the labour and delivery ward, then backtrack, move left instead. Mostly I was pushed along these hallways on a gurney or in a wheelchair — my bearings aren't dependable. I skate past the entry to the NICU, not quite looking and not quite avoiding, turn down the next narrow hallway, take another right, find myself at the end of the hallway I've been seeking, glass doors like dominoes all along one side.

The last door is Helen's. I'm eager to see her again, in need of her kindness, her honesty. I'm in need of her ability to reflect me too. She belongs at the cusp of this new story — she witnessed our lives along that crease of time which is everywhere and nowhere from here. My hands are sweating. I wonder how much she will remember, how much I will forget.

Helen has heard me coming, I suppose, and she meets me at the door, arms open. I walk into her firm embrace, feel all the exhausting work of translation drop away, three months of navigating between ordinary world and extraordinary suffering, between what I know and what I cannot say. Helen knows. She meets me where I am, and holds me a long time.

A one-year-old child will kiss a sad face in a storybook, so perhaps it's a basic impulse to touch an aching soul, an instinct to comfort. Touch can't mend what is broken, can't retrieve what is lost, but it is profoundly restorative all the same. It offers some assurance of continuing citizenship in the big world. It says, *I will wait.* In this instant's swamp of memory, the strength of Helen's presence makes all the difference.

We break apart, smile awkwardly as we dab at our eyes, then settle into conversation. It's an odd connection: beyond that most harrowing event of my life, Helen knows almost nothing about me, and I know even less about her. The occasion for shy self-declarations hurtled past us like the tail of a comet, flint and gravel pinging off the ticking moments.

We talk now, and it's effortless. She tells me about her teenage daughter, a swimmer. She asks about Bill, about my mom. The office is tiny, filled to capacity with Helen's life, her energy. I feel safe. She leans forward in her chair, searches me out. *How are you, Charlene?*

The question is familiar, and the inflection too: generous sympathy and concern. But here, in the disconcerting shadows of a baby's life, it's a genuine invitation. This woman knows something of bereaved mothers; she can meet me on a different patch of ground.

I breathe in, and begin. *I'm sad, I'm sad a lot. I'm not back to work — thank God for that, I'm so relieved you helped me to find that option. I'm not at work, and I'm not missing it. I don't know what I do, really.*

Something has shaken loose, a rattle of language; I feel it clattering down this steep grade. *But I don't have much clarity for big tasks, and I'm not really interested in company — it's too much work to buoy myself up, to be sociable. I don't really care about others' lives just now; I don't feel like I want to bother.*

I pause for air, resolve to stop and fail. *I'm not reading much, I don't have the concentration or the interest, and all the stuff about grieving just seems so banal, so silly. My mom and I talk on the phone — I think she's worried I might be depressed.*

Depressed. The word hangs there, suspended by invisible fishing line, turning slowly so that we can consider it from every angle.

Do you feel depressed? She asks the question gently, without judgment.

I'm sad, I say. *I'm sad but I actually don't think I'm depressed. It's thick, this walk through sorrow, and I'm certainly not clear of it yet. Some days I wonder how long it might take, but I don't know — I think I'm just sad. What do you think?*

She sits a moment, thinking. *Mothers worry,* she says. She is here, holding my mother, holding me, and she is elsewhere, thinking about mothering her own daughter. *Your mother is far away, and that's hard for her. She would do anything to comfort you, we both know that. She wants you to find your way back to sturdiness, and she wants you to have help if you need it. This is a mother's ground zero, Charlene, and you know it yourself from your time in Chloe's company: you would have done anything to release her from some of that difficulty, to assume the suffering in her stead. It's not even rational, that need to intervene, to relieve your child's misery.*

We look at one another a long time. I'm plotting myself onto the map of mothers, assuming my rites of initiation. Helen is quiet, watchful. When the moment arrives, she says, *What do you need, do you think?*

I don't know. Time. I need time. I need time and lots of space to cry.

Take it, Charlene. Keep asking yourself, keep answering yourself. Do what you need. She reaches across the space between us, places a hand on my arm. *Be patient. Reassure your mother, and come back, if you wish — I'd like that.*

On my way to the elevator a few minutes later, I step into the NICU, let myself be surrounded by the beeps and whirs of this one-time home.

EACH DAY ON HIS WALK to and from the campus, Bill passes the memorial tree. He pauses, gathers his heart for the day. This is his Chloe time, his chance to reorient the forces that shape his present. *Sometimes I bury my face in the needles,* he tells me. *I like the sharpness against my skin.* As winter fades, friends and family begin to claim the cards from the tree. One day I notice Chloe's nestled amongst the dried petals in our room. Bill has tied a white ribbon from the tree to the zipper of his coat.

Painstakingly, we claim our Chloe spaces. One afternoon I gather all the dried blooms into a clear crystal vase and set it on the dresser in our room. Their scent still lingers, and the softened colours rustle against one another. I carry the birth announcement into an art shop and meet a woman who takes time to search out the right mat and frame. We hang the little footprints near the fragile petals, then add the angel from my sister. It's not a shrine we're looking for, but a quiet space, protected from the rush of living.

I think of my friend saying she will hold open a space for me while I'm in the depths of mourning. I can see that I am holding open a space for my daughter. Am I hoping she will return? Not exactly. I am hoping that time will teach me who she is, and how I can know her. I am hoping to discern what eludes me.

I am facing a tribunal. In front of me are three babies, and I must choose. These are the rules; I understand them all too well. The first is only a stick, inert. It is not my baby. The second is a doll, wrapped in flannel. It is a child's baby, readied for pretend worlds. The third is a real baby, naked and bloodied. She is the one I recognize, she is mine. I stand a long time. I will take the pretend baby, I say. I have washed my share of miniature clothes; I can almost love a doll. I pause, consider my decision. I will return for the dead baby, I say. I speak carefully, emphatically. I cannot hold her yet. I will return for her when I'm strong, when I'm able.

AT LEAST ONCE A WEEK, I meet my friend Brenda for lunch. We slough off our bulky coats, squash mitts and scarves into sleeves, then settle into our favourite booth. It's quiet here, and the light is delicate. Brenda reaches across the table, squeezes my hand. *How are you?* she asks. She's a searching woman, a force. I am relieved to be in her presence.

Truthfully, I'm not good. I've had days now with more ease than anguish, better balance, but today is not one of them. Today I am grim, holding on for dear life. I peer toward her through the tunnel of my dark self. *Not good,* I say.

I should have stayed home. I would have stayed home, but I'm afraid to be alone with myself, afraid of this headlong pitch into grey ash.

Hm, she says. *What is it, do you think?*

I know perfectly well what it is. I'm a toxic waste site, a woman mired in sorrow. I am poor company. I am needy and distressed and self-absorbed. I am mourning and mourning, and I fear I may never find an end to this agony. I am a woman who apparently cannot accept that she has lost her child. I thought I was coping, but I am not. I am a failure.

I don't know, really — the same old thing. I sound petulant, but I don't feel it. I'm embarrassed, ashamed, exhausted. I'm at a loss.

She gazes at me. She's calm, generous, sympathetic. She's also entirely separate from me. *It's Chloe?* Her voice is gentle. I feel it float through the sun that slants across the table, register the instant it reaches me, soft like the sudden perfume of sweet peas. I hunch over the table and nod. *Yes: Chloe.*

For a long time, a survivor dwells in the moment the ship wrecks. The catastrophe defines her and dwarfs her. Weeks after a wreck, though, she begins to chafe: how long should disaster have life-shaping power? Could it become a sorcery, obliterating the person who stood calmly on the deck beforehand?

Tell me, Brenda says.

I do. I tell her that I am pummelled by grief. I am so bereft today that I can hardly move, I can hardly speak. I tell her that I am failing: I thought I was moving along the echoing corridor, but now I am back where I started, with no air in my lungs, no sense of where I am going, no recollection of what I am supposed to do on the way. I am pinned to the moment of the shattered heart. I bleed tears.

Brenda listens. She listens, she prompts, she makes a space among the half-empty plates for my lament. I'm not the first survivor she's cared for. She knows how to offer tea and tenderness, and fearless intuition. She waits while the echoes play themselves out, settle into silence.

I gaze at this thing I've placed between us, a tangle of crushed hopes and self-censure, exhaustion, fear, hope. I straighten up, look across at my friend.

It feels to you like you're stuck, she says finally, *like you're caught in an endless repetition.*

My throat is too tight to talk. I nod.

She smiles, reaches across to me. *I don't hear it,* she says, *I don't hear that at all. Every time you tell me the story of Chloe, the story of losing Chloe, it's different from the last time you told it. I hear you moving through your sorrow, and—how can I put this?—it's like your story moves with you.*

I watch her carefully. I'm dubious: that is today's poison. But I do trust her—I trust her better than myself. I pause, searching through this vision she is offering.

Then relief floods up from somewhere. Everything shifts just slightly, and in the midst of the chaos of my mourning, in the midst of the suffocation, sorrow, paralytic fear, I see a woman determined to hold her infant, a woman struggling to find the courage to call herself mother. This woman rehearses and rehearses, hoping to find a story she can live with since she cannot get the story she wants. She hovers there, above the wreck in the icy water. Making a space for one who is gone requires all the time and patience she can muster.

One of my jobs is to honour that mother, the way she honours her baby. It's a big task.

March 1996

AFTER MONTHS OF PHYSICAL STRUGGLE, I slam headfirst into a wall of frustration. My right hip joint has seized up, making it hard to climb stairs and almost impossible to get in and out of the car. My diaphragm spasms several times a day, pulling me rigid with pain. I'm reluctant to walk anywhere on my own because I am not sure I'll be able to get back.

My limits tighten around me. I feel incapacitated and anxious. I have always been a healthy, vigorous woman who walks and laughs and moves easily in the world. I'm no longer this person. I'm not at home in this fragile, unreliable body.

My medical team doesn't have much to offer. The surgeon points out he could open me up again, but the trauma of another surgery might only compound the problem. Patience and persistence, that is their counsel. It seems precious little.

One of my friends recommends massage therapy. I am surprised not to have thought of it myself. I'm not certain it will do much to address my physical challenges, but I know it will calm and comfort me. I ask around for recommendations, make an appointment. When I arrive, I puzzle over the health history form with its diagrammed body. I mark the hip joint, the zone around my rib cage. I consider circling the heart and drawing a jagged crack across it. Where do I draw the dull ache that chills all my days?

The massage therapist glances at the paper, then leads me into her quiet room, gestures toward the massage table, then excuses herself while I undress and stretch out. A row of heat lamps warms the air above my body. As I settle, I realize how tense I am. I am shy about this encounter — it takes a lot of nerve to bring my vulnerable self into close contact with someone who doesn't know what I am struggling with these days.

But some of the tension in me comes from caring for my husband and family and friends and students, all of whom feel their own sorrow and bewilderment in the wake of this death. Some comes from being out in public spaces where mothers push strollers or scold intractable toddlers or absent-mindedly smooth their own promising bellies. Some is the amorphous sadness about my miscarriage. Some comes from inhabiting a body that is so slow to mend.

The massage therapist knocks lightly and enters. She is older than I had anticipated, an athletic woman, perhaps late fifties. She exudes a certain efficiency: whatever is locked in me, she'll find and release. I'm not a newcomer to massage, but still I'm surprised by how good it feels. Heat, pressure, the rhythm of breathing — and the relief of letting down the barriers that protect me from accidental assault. I begin to relax for the first time in weeks.

At first we exchange a word here and there, but as she eases into her work, this woman begins to talk. She details the benefits of modalities like massage as an important part of maintaining good health. I murmur my agreement, but I'm not very engaged — I would be happier to disappear from words here on this table. My muscles trigger and release under her hands.

She is just getting warmed up. She talks about other alternative therapies, and her tone becomes less casual: she is instructing me, I can feel a reprimand sitting just below the surface. My eyebrows knit together. I am naked on a table in a strange room being lectured by someone I don't know. I feel exposed, uncomfortable.

And then I feel trapped. *Bearing babies is a natural phenomenon*, she says. *Women have babies — they have always had babies. Women in other times had babies in the fields, babies in their homes. They didn't complicate the process.*

I wince. Complication, hazard — this is what I know. I don't want her to talk about this, I don't want to listen.

It's only in our time that we have decided pregnancy and childbirth need to be managed by doctors.

I had more medical intervention than I would have wished, but it was hardly optional.

We create risk for women and their infants by turning pregnancy and childbirth into a medical experience. Women have healthy babies if they're just allowed to follow the wisdom of their own bodies.

My mind roars away into a cavern of self-doubt, self-recrimination. If I had chosen more natural care for myself, then maybe my baby would be alive, and I would be the joyful mother who ghosts me every waking moment.

I come screaming back to myself. If I had chosen more natural care, I would be dead, an explosion of blood vessels. Both my baby and I would be dead, leaving an even bigger vortex of grief in our wake.

I retreat as far as I can from the hectoring voice. *How dare you*, I want to say. *You have no idea*, I want to say. *You are hurting me*, I want to say. Pinned down by anger, vulnerability, and crippling codes of politeness, I say nothing. An agonizing half-hour later, I gather my wits and my last shreds of dignity, and leave the office, swearing under my breath never ever to return. It's small consolation.

Then I weep for days. I feel scalded by her comments, but I also recognize their seductive power. *If only I had, if only I hadn't*: these are tripwires for me, familiar but treacherous. My temptation hovers around that point of catastrophe, then lures me with other narratives that would accomplish my heart's desire. Self-recrimination waits in the shadows, arms wide, to break my fall.

If I could claim responsibility, perhaps I could understand the terrible sentence I have been dealt. Another if.

IN SPITE OF THE EMOTIONAL HAVOC, it's only a few days before I begin to experience improvements in my mobility. My hip joint still complains but has a much broader range of motion. My diaphragm is easing out too — it seizes up only a couple of times a day. I feel stronger, and I'm certain the changes are connected with the deep muscle work on that massage table. Hope and dread begin a curious dance: this woman might help to heal me, but can I bear the pain in that healing?

Finally I talk it out with one of my friends who points out that I'm responding well to the therapy but not to the therapist — why don't I ask around and try someone else? I surprise us both by laughing out loud. It's so reasonable, and I've been too blocked to see it. I have been caught up in the mythology that healing hurts, and another assumption that hums underneath that one: I deserve to suffer.

I wonder how many mothers have felt trapped here, extending and deepening their own suffering. I begin to make some calls.

WHEN I MEET AMANDA, I am both more cautious and more determined. If she is not the right healer for me, I will try another and another. I fidget over the same health history form, finally circle the whole body. On the blank lines, I write: *Severe pre-eclampsia in November, premature baby who died. Gallbladder attacks in January, surgery in February. Injured hip joint, spasming diaphragm, high blood pressure, broken heart.*

When I pass it to her, I feel exposed, but also defiant. This is my truth; I want her to know it. Her eyes scan the page, she shakes her head. *This must be such a sad time for you,* she says. She stands, breathes deeply, leads me into a place that will become my sanctuary.

We speak very little that first day. Apart from making sure I'm warm enough, she asks nothing of me. She knows I am in mourning — she seems to understand my distance from the world. I feel safe. I also feel anonymous. I know nothing of this woman's life or friends or worries, and she knows nothing of mine. I feel her warm hands and the calm force of her presence, but she is focused on my over-taxed body. I have the sensation of release — I am unfettered, I drift in the calm of the room. The hour is fleeting, like a sigh. I walk home and sleep for hours.

I visit Amanda frequently for several weeks. It's true: my body does respond well to massage therapy. My hip joint eases out and my diaphragm begins to loosen up too. It's hard work, and we share it between us. She works intently and patiently, and I follow her hands, do what I can at the levels beneath consciousness to unlock knots and injuries.

Some of the work is clear. The muscles and tendons around my hip need a lot of attention, and I learn to expect a couple of days of tenderness after a session. Some of our shared moments are more surprising. On one early visit, we pause together at an explosion of pain along my backbone. It knocks the air out of me. Amanda holds her warm hands in position until the tension unlocks. I am swept back to the delivery room, and realize we're attending to the spot where needles pierced my spine. It's a curious sensation, like visiting ghosts in a museum of bones and muscle.

Even more curious to me is how often I am flooded by intense emotion when we trip over these sites. Tears, laughter, guilt, anger, wonder, terrible fatigue: they erupt from somewhere outside consciousness. I am without script, without reason. I spill out feeling because Amanda is safe for me. I know she can shake it off before she leaves this room.

Together, we wander through my bewildering museum, broken and vital. She asks nothing of me. She attends to my journey in a way I could not attend to my own daughter's journey. She teaches me to forgive myself. I arrive at the end of each hour feeling exhausted and cleansed.

As the snow disappears, Bill and I begin to walk. At first it's slow. We walk two blocks, and I grip his arm, grateful for the support. We pick up lattes in Styrofoam cups, head back home again. It takes a long time; my bones complain.

One Sunday late in March, we set out on a longer walk: I want to see the memorial tree. We are buoyed by the water trickling along the curbs, the swelling buds on tree branches. By the time we walk the curving road into the park, I am beginning to tire. We seem a long way from home. We crest the hill, and are confronted by the noise of families, their rowdy jubilation at being out in the soft air. I clutch Bill's arm, a desperate, empty woman, bent over with longing. He reaches across, places his hand on mine. *Nearly there*, he says quietly.

Between a cage of squalling peacocks and another of prolific rabbits, our tree is busy with its own life. Long tips of new growth, vivid green, punctuate each branch. They are firm but soft, like the feet of young cats. I stand for a moment on the sidewalk, wondering how to meet a tree which is, by odd luck, an intimate part of our uncommon family. I step into it, breathe in its smell. My cheeks are wet with tears.

Bill and I sit together on the nearby bench — my body needs to rest. We watch a small boy throw handful after handful of gravel on the metal slide, captivated by the noise, astonished that he can make it himself. He is one of many children here. Not one of them is mine. I am mesmerized by the gleeful boy. Every second bruises me, yet I cannot tear my attention away.

Then it's time. We walk the small hill, and I look back at Chloe's tree. A light lived there, a spirit clings. We pass Betsy's front steps on the long walk home.

OUT OF GRIEF, SINGING

April 1996 – Present

Grief is love, I suppose. Love as a backwards glance.

— Helen Humphreys

Spring 1996

IN SOUTHERN ONTARIO, winter's end doesn't test your faith the way it does on the prairies. The grass is already green when the snow begins to disappear, and magnolia trees swell with buds long before they should. Black-clad Mennonite farmers bring new maple syrup to the Saturday morning market in their horse-drawn carts. People wander along the rows of stalls, consider hard-crusted sourdough bread, cheese curd, sausages. Hands emerge from mittens, reach for apples and carrots kept crisp in someone's barn. We laugh at the flower-seller's outrageous banter, return to our cars with paper cones of daisies, carnations, roses, freesia. It's our communal celebration, a forward remembering.

I can manoeuvre again. My hip joint supports me, and I can't remember the last time I was immobilized by a spasming diaphragm. I meander through the crowds, riding the current of my own good health. Hope is like sap: I'm returning to life, along with everything else.

Bill and I map larger and larger circles when we head out to walk. We retrace familiar routes, we turn down new streets. It's a project, it's a pleasure. We walk through the evenings, watch lawns and flowers emerge from slush, tricycles and basketball hoops from dusty garages. Just the two of us, taking stock of where we are now, in the lengthening days when breath balances sorrow.

We like it best at the edge of dark — hush, privacy, ease. We glimpse heads bent over homework, the blue glow of a television, a person leaning against the window, absorbed in a phone conversation. We catch a scrap of cello on still air, or a flute, the rattle of drums. We lift these moments out of other lives, carry them with us. We're in search of something, a way to understand home. We are a family of two, we are a family of three. We are warmer in our sadness.

One evening we find ourselves at the brick archway of the sprawling old cemetery many blocks from home. We hesitate, then wander the paths, leaning down to feel the inscriptions on tiny headstones. Some of these stones have stood here whispering their stories for more than a century and a half. A single child, a cluster of children, lives ended after a few days, a few months, a few years. *Fanny, beloved daughter of. John, young son and brother of. Esther. Wilhelm.* Even the moss travelling their surfaces is eloquent. We sit on a bench in the rapidly cooling evening and realize that we've shaken free of our trepidation. We've left it along the gravel trails, walked it into the grass.

Evening follows evening. The magnolia trees burst into bloom, then apples, cherries, lilacs. We walk, hand in hand, through dark air shattered by blossoms.

As spring performs its green invasion, I begin to write again. I've never been a disciplined writer, so it's not the rituals around writing that I've been missing. It's something far more unsettling: I've been removed from my own words. Language has had little traction in my grief world, and without it, I've been reeling through unfamiliar landscapes, doubly disoriented. A writer without words — it's been a painful estrangement.

After adjusting to months of inner silence, I start to hear fragments again—a word or two, spinning in the light. One evening, I disappear into my study, put myself in the way of them. Small shards of language, cool, crystalline. I collect them, piece them together until they show me a woman, numbed with loss, held in place by fence posts marching across the winter prairie. I work the syllables hard: I want to feel the brittle air, I want to feel the stunned heart.

In the quiet of my study, I am both the aching woman and the labouring writer. My language is strong enough now to ferry me—I travel back and forth for hours. When I settle back in my chair, the light is draining out of the day. I am exhilarated. I don't even realize that my face is wet with tears.

IN MAY, MOM AND DAD COME OUT to share a week of spring weather with us. On Mother's Day, the four of us load into the car and head for Lake Huron, a blue expanse, a space like prairie. We're escaping the threat of suffocation, the slow spill of hours.

I glance at Mom, watch her scanning this landscape. Her eyes settle on the aging barns, the stands of maple, the curving undulations so different from the flatness coursing in our veins. In the rear-view mirror, I can see Dad and Bill dozing in the back seat, a pair of fathers connected not through blood but through the ease of sleep. The car hums through the green, a small sphere cradling adult parents, adult children.

We come around another bend and the road opens out ahead of us, straight as a section line. Mom and I both gasp at the sudden familiarity. Two minutes later, we are in a tunnel of trees, a mile or more, tall arms reaching across to meet one another. Shelter belts don't grow like this where we come from. The ghost of home dissipates as suddenly as it appeared, shreds of smoke in a stiff wind.

We track across the curving skin of earth, our eyes lingering on patches of tender new corn. Water lies heavy in too many fields, machines abandoned at the edge of workable land. Spring this year is a haze of new green spinning away from the stranglehold of black muck. New growth, residual damage — I belong here.

All afternoon, we meander through small towns scattered along the shore of the big lake. We have time to be curious. We get as close as we can to an antique jail, contemplate ghosts behind the old brick. We gaze into shop windows in summer resort towns. We scramble down rickety steps to walk a stretch of stony beach. Boats bump against the piers while the cottages above them await a flood of sun and air. Almost nobody is around today. We're left alone to explore a forthcoming world.

It's suppertime when we turn onto another main street in another village, and park in front of the local hotel. We've arranged to meet a distant cousin of my father's. We push open the front door and find ourselves in a dining room packed with people. It takes me a minute to realize that all of these families are here to celebrate their mothers, treating them to meals they haven't had to prepare. We weave through the narrow channels between tables, and find the man and his wife, along with the woman's aged mother, at a table near the back.

I can feel my tension rising now. I feel crowded by the heavy smells, the chipped Arborite tabletops, the uncooperative chairs. I'm uncomfortable with the ceremony of this meal. But our hosts are unassuming. They talk of the unusual winter weather and the wet spring. They talk of their lives here: the orchard, the tourists, local politics. My parents remember other reunions in other places, trace branches of their family tree. The tightness in me begins to ease. I remember the goodness of shared food, of being in the company of decent people. Bill sits next to me, leaning toward the old woman across the table. The harried waitress brings our plates. Curls of steam from my potatoes tangle with the steam trails from other plates. There is kinship here and I am safe enough.

We cut our roast beef into small squares, stab at the carrots with their scatter of chopped parsley. We eat, we talk, we feel the energy circling through this cramped restaurant. The waitress clears away our plates and offers pie: apple, cherry, raisin. I wonder, idly, why I've never mastered the art of pastry. We drink weak coffee or strong tea, settle back in our hard seats.

The backdrop of noise shifts. The first wave of diners leaves, and several tables are now wiped clean and waiting. As we contemplate the bottom of our cups, the waitress returns. Her arm reaches across in front of me, deposits a foil-wrapped chocolate. *For the mothers*, she says brightly, expectation warming her voice. She produces one for each woman at our table.

My eyes flick up in terror, catch my mom's glance, drop again to this brilliant bauble. *For the mothers, for the mothers*: it's a chant, a child's rhyme, a torment. I am not a mother. I am a failed mother. I am an invisible mother.

I would veer away from this accident, but I can't break free of the force field of these women. My mother and the old woman — they sit with their daughters. But the daughters? Their stories are less clear. In this instant, the mystery and scope of mothering lock all four of us together, a puzzle of interconnected metal rings.

We're frozen for a long second in our awkward postures, cement-coated bodies hardened in mid-reach. Then the old woman raises her face to the waitress, offers a gracious word, begins to peel back the shining red foil from her chocolate heart. The gesture releases us. Breath returns to everyone at the table, all that is unspoken remains safely wrapped in silence.

Mother's Day, my first one. I have a gaping hole where a child should be. Still, the ragged edges are no longer bleeding. The daughter of the old woman has no children either. I wonder what secrets she pulls close to her each night at the edge of sleep.

Before we leave, we spend a patient minute unwrapping our hearts, taste sweetness on our tongues.

I AM ALWAYS AMAZED by the rampant growth in my adopted home — my own garden scripts come from a less hospitable climate. As May gives way to June, I scissor away at the forsythia and the zealous hedges, pluck out determined grape hyacinth bulbs before they take over. If a person needed proof that living things want nothing more than to perpetuate life, a garden is a perfect lesson.

I tend my garden, but half-heartedly. It's not so much that I don't have the strength. It's more that I lack the desire. The life force is bursting forth all around me — it hardly seems right to thwart it.

I throw open the windows in my study and let the spring air waft through. Often, I find myself abandoning my shears and gloves halfway through a gardening task and disappearing into the shaded tangle of words instead. I'm ready to revisit the bloom of pregnancy, a time before terror, a time of extravagant joy. Reclaiming that innocence feels risky, but in the face of my irrepressible garden, refusing it seems wrong-headed.

The growing things lift my spirits. I carry armfuls of flowers into my house. I flop into my deck chair and read in the sun. I write poems of big-bellied wonder. I surrender myself to the gentle potency of the green world.

Living things may be fragile, but life itself is powerful.

Summer 1996

A FRIEND CALLS FROM WINNIPEG with a proposal: she wants to
drive to New York City, and she wants me to come with her. New
York is a long way from Manitoba — far like the moon. But it's
only one long day's drive from my Ontario home. She will pick me
up, and we'll spend some days adventuring.

We soak up the city in all the ways I like best. We traipse
along the crowded streets, wander through shops, sit in outdoor
cafés. We take the subway, then locate ourselves on the crumpled
maps we pull from our bags. We are lazy, time is loose.

After an afternoon immersing ourselves in the grand beauty
of the Metropolitan Museum, I want postcards to send to my
friends. My eyes skate over the huge wall of possibilities in the gift
shop, and I begin to assemble a deck in my hand. I'm visiting my
own interior caves as I select these images, and I'm connecting
myself with people I care about. It strikes me that I am actually
strong again.

My hand hovers like a divining rod along a row of van
Goghs. I hesitate over a pencil sketch, grey on grey, so different
from the blotches of colour around it. I pull it from the rack and
study it. A seated woman curls over her own knees, head resting
on arms, face buried. She is supported by nothing more solid than
cross-hatching and the suggestion of light, yet she sits heavily, feet
planted against the ground, legs muscled but not tensing toward
movement. Her hair falls along the ridges of her spine, her breasts
hang. I notice her soft belly. A hand, her right, appears from
under her left arm. Resting lightly on her thigh, it betrays nothing
about the woman whose eyes are hidden from me, except that she
cannot reach for anything, for anyone. Her ear, unobscured by
hair, hovers like a promise.

Only a thin pencil line protects the privacy of this solitary
being. Inscribed, carefully and sturdily in the lower right hand

corner, is a single word: *Sorrow*. Title, definition, condition. It's underlined.

The glittering gift shop falls away, and I am alone with a woman whose eyes avoid everything, a woman who journeys inward to find something she cannot imagine. Her body is closed. She will not open her mouth, her eyes, her arms toward me. She will not stand and walk. She doesn't flinch away — she simply cares nothing for me. Absorbed in her own hell, she is too busy to care. She's full to the brim, Sorrow is. Company is taxing when you're overfull.

I gaze at the woman, and at the word that names her. They know nothing of one another, and they know only one another: that puzzle holds me hostage. I look at her a long time.

Then I lean toward her, whisper my own name into her ear. I want to remind her to drink in the stillness, and then to stretch her legs, walk past the frame that binds her in that featureless space, open her arms to me. We could, I think, comfort one another. I whisper my name, hear it echo against cool cave walls.

BEFORE THE SUMMER ENDS and we must return to our classrooms, Bill and I escape together. We don't travel often, but we travel well — both of us love the privacy of our little car, the open time to speak about whatever comes to the surface. We gather our camping gear, and head for Cape Breton.

On big roads and small, we cross half the continent. We swear at uncooperative tent poles, we laugh about bad coffee, we fill our eyes in mist-soaked lake country. We talk about where we've been — the people who've helped us, the people who've compounded our pain, the concern we've felt for one another. We talk about the future too. Bill is contemplating a return to school. If he added nursing training to his cell biology background, he could shift his research specialization to embrace neonatal health. It's exactly the right next step — a perfect way to express Chloe's imprint.

The days drift by and finally we rumble across the long causeway that attaches the rest of Canada to Cape Breton Island. The landscape rolling away in front of us is green and wild — and old, very old. It's also unusually hot. When we stop for gas, the weather is the topic for the locals clustered over half-empty cups. *Supposed to get up into the 90s again this afternoon,* they say, shaking their heads in amazement. *Can't remember the last time we had this kind of heat wave in August.*

Bill and I drive the winding highways. We're sweating in the captivity of our car, but the ocean air is decent compensation, and anyway, we're adventuring. In a scant few hours, we'll have our tent up and be settling back with a cold drink.

It works like that too. We find a shaded site, then spend an hour walking the coast, picking up rocks that predate humanity. Later, we eat food out of cans because we can't imagine building a fire, and we melt into our camp chairs, our hands smudging the pages of our books. Eventually we collapse into sleep in the muggy air of our tent.

The next day is the same. Everyone languishes in the heat. Only the ice cream stand an hour down the highway is doing a brisk business. Bill and I drift through the hours, expending as little effort as possible. By late afternoon, our curiosity about this place outweighs our lethargy. We fill a couple of water bottles, pick up a park map, and set off on one of the short trails.

Almost immediately, we're inside the tumult of old forest — dark air and that ripe smell, growth and mould. We can almost hear the endless cycling of elements: carbon, nitrogen, hydrogen, oxygen. We step thoughtfully over giant roots. We're at the base of a green mountain. We could see its bald spot on our way to the trailhead. Eventually our path will take us mostly up, but at the moment, we rise and dip, curve around thick stands of trees, stretch our arms into the green space beneath the limbs of these enormous trees.

It *is* hot. We pause for water. My breathing is already audible. I don't have much stamina yet, but my hip is not complaining. And we have all the time in the world.

A creek races toward us, then veers off and bumps down the stream bed behind us. We walk through green humidity. I stop more often than I'd like to, and lean against a tree or the rails of a bridge. I need to catch my breath. The trail hugs the creek now, so we can watch it dance through deeps and shallows. It's impossible to talk over the racket, but we move and pause in concert, connected by the rhythm of our walking, by the history we carry between us. We are gentle, here in this unfamiliar wild place. We are reaching toward one another, stretching toward a future.

Partway up the hill, our path veers away from the creek. Everything is sharper in the sudden silence — the startle of birdsong, the sound of our own breath. We pause on the incline, peer out through the green, catch a glint of sun on the faraway ocean. We're suspended, halfway up a mountain, in the warmth of a dream.

The climb is gruelling, especially for a mending body. I lean on my stick, I chant myself forward through the hot air. Truthfully, I don't mind the effort, the whine of over-challenged joints, the pull of air to the bottom of tight lungs. We climb and we climb. We curve around the back edge of this wooded mountain and then suddenly burst into sun, wind, the stretch of sky. It's astonishing, the world.

A mountaintop laughs at the confines of skin. It dreams immensities, sings bigger songs. We stand, two small bodies on a flat-topped mountain, and contemplate ageless rock, an ageless forest, the ageless sea. We pull off our hats and shake out our hair in the limitless sky. Golden eagles draw lazy circles far above us. The ocean reaches toward and away. We are minuscule, but we know ourselves to be a part of this grand old world, folded into the pleats of its apron. We belong here. Birds speak to us, the wind has language. There is room, here, for our terror, our fear, our sorrow. There is room here for our wishing.

We lie back on the grass and study the thin sky. We stay a long time, riveted by circling eagles. The ocean shifts and shifts far below us, and the air begins to cool, just slightly. My breathing slows to normal, and then slows again, air pushed deep by awe. Finally, we are ready to begin the trek back to earth, to the lives awaiting us there. We stand together clasping hands for a long minute, then begin.

The trail leads us around a clump of berry bushes, and then another. We come tight around the third curve, and a small rabbit sits directly in front of us. I stop, Bill bumps into me. *Look —*

The rabbit looks at us too, then returns to its patient meal of bark. It hitches forward, takes stock of the greenery, hitches back again. We wait. A minute ticks past, and another. We take a step forward. The rabbit appraises us, moves away. We step forward, and it disappears into the brush. The trail dodges more berry patches, then arrives at a meadow, and there is the rabbit again, sitting ahead of us on the trail, waiting.

At least we think it is waiting, and it might be true.

This rabbit is dark brown, with whispers of white. The rabbit in our minds is small and white, with downy fur and drooping ears. It kept watch, silently, hour upon hour, in Chloe's isolette. Chloe's bunny. It has, we realize, become a shorthand for us. Quick and elusive, small, improbably sturdy: the idea of it helps us to know a daughter who exists for us in semaphore, two lost adults waving across a gulf of sorrow.

The brown rabbit guides us on our journey down the mountain. It points out the finest bark, the hollows which offer privacy and a quick rest. It twitches its whiskers in exactly the right combination to heave open the locked chambers of our broken selves. Green air and hope pour in, we feel the slight sting of salt.

A COUPLE OF DAYS LATER, we meet Captain Rick. He stands on the deck of his old boat in worn sandals, ball cap pulled low over his eyes. This is his water: his gaze rubs across it, tender, like a hand on velvet. He is searching for the whales who play here these days. He has loaded up his boat with tourists and is taking us to meet these creatures he loves.

I wonder if he finds us appalling, a gauche and awkward insertion into this landscape. I watch his eyes move. His body relaxes into the lilt of the boat. He is at home here; we are visitors. I twist to look over the side of the boat. The water froths away from us. I raise my eyes, squint into the sunshine, register the warmth of the afternoon.

Captain Rick's gaze stiffens suddenly, and he cranks the wheel, surges across the neck of this inlet. Two minutes later, he cuts the power, and we're rocking in the sharp silence. Cameras emerge, chatter crackles through the group. Whales, we're going to see whales.

Pilot whales are barely bigger than dolphins. They are lithe and playful, and in these August days they're enjoying the coast of Cape Breton, as we are. The cluster of humans waits in high anticipation. The pod of whales circles toward us, brave and curious. We see them blowing, point to the spot just as it vanishes.

When one breaches near the boat, a flurry of excitement breaks out. I grab Bill's sleeve and bounce on my toes, giddy as a child. Another whale breaches and blows, and a sound comes hurtling out of my throat. I wonder if I will faint from sheer joy. I hadn't anticipated this, the acute pleasure, the surprise, the wonder. Their bodies are smooth, strong, slick with water. For the first five minutes, every display for our floating boatload is a miracle, and then we begin to relax into the rhythm of it. We wonder if this is the same whale as the one that breached just there, and oh, one just dived under the boat — can you see it on your side? We are less stunned, and we laugh rather than gasp.

Then a mother breaches, a young calf tucked in next to her. The two of them lift and dive, lift again. From that moment, I can see nothing but them — this mother, this child, their pas de deux through the water. They breach and dive, over and over, and finally surface and nuzzle. I wonder what she is telepathing with her powerful body. Praise and pleasure? Caution? Attention? I wonder if it's always been so easy, the perfect synchrony of two bodies, a large one and a small one, lifting and lowering, lifting and lowering.

Watching them play here in this protected inlet, I taste the primal innocence of the maternal story — the young asserting, *You are my mother*, inventing the potency of the mother, offering something like courage. The mother, in turn, assumes the role she is afforded by this strange fate of connection. She will coax and counsel, teach and tax and torment. She will ease her baby into the proprieties of this underwater culture. She will worry this being toward adulthood.

But not now. At this very moment, this mother and this calf are absorbed in their play. They dance together, a choreography scored right into their genes. They are revelling, here, with only a handful of humans to witness them.

I lean toward this mother. My shoulders ache with concentration. I want, more than anything, to thank her in a language she might understand.

Autumn 1996

THE FALL ARRIVES, and both Bill and I are more calm, more steady. Teaching is demanding, but I am interested in ideas again, and energized by the conversation in my classrooms. My students circle around me shyly — my experience has tested their innocence too. My colleagues are considerate. They bolster me when my spirits flag, but leave me lots of room to strengthen my nerve. I feel welcomed. My days have shape and meaning, and I am less afraid of where I have been, where I am going.

My nights offer a different vantage point. Sometimes I sleep quietly, but more often I am tangled in gnarled narratives of lost treasures, spoiled feasts, wrecked buildings, erratic weather, rash bargains.

One night I dream of a muffled voice, calling and calling. I have a familiar tightness in my throat: terror. I run up and down a maze of hallways, rattling doorknobs and peering in dusty storage closets. I am desperate to locate the voice — it is growing faint. A custodian with a jangling ring of keys appears, fumbles with a lock. As the door swings open, I shoulder past him, clamber over upturned chairs and old theatre props. Behind the clutter is an ornate sarcophagus, levered open, a person toppling out as I watch. I am stricken. I race to catch him, feel the fiery heat of his body collapsing against me. *Almost dead,* I think. *I hope I am not too late.*

I drift near waking until my breathing evens out. I wonder about the fainting man, the terrible heat. And the sarcophagus? Such elaborate trappings for the dead, such suffocating entrapment for the living.

I head to my computer to catch the bits and pieces before they evaporate. Even in the early days when I was so divorced from my own language, I transcribed the big nightmares. Partly I was defusing their potency — dream fear can trail me for hours. More than that, these dreams carried such an air of consequence that they demanded attention. They felt like encrypted messages from the part of me that was hiding from daylight. Even in the first weeks after Chloe's death, I wanted to capture them, keep them safe until I had the strength to hear them fully.

I scratch out some notes about the collapsing stranger, hesitate a long moment, then open the folder and read through all the strange fables that I have caught and caged over the past months. Some I remember vividly, some are almost new to me. I linger over them, appreciating their economy and their blunt terror. Then I push away from my desk, find my way into the world of light.

I MOVE MOSTLY THROUGH NETWORKS OF ADULTS, and I am grateful for that. For the first time in my life, I am skittish around young kids. Not so much the children of my friends and colleagues, but all the others — the ones galloping past me in the grocery aisle, the ones holding court in their strollers, faces covered with banana mush. I see children everywhere, each of them dense with mystery. I stand on the periphery of their universe, feel my fingers tightening around the chain link fence that forbids my entrance.

On All Hallow's Eve, I can't avoid them — our neighbourhood is alive with cats and ladybugs, goblins and princesses and robots. I am both thrilled and anxious about meeting these innocents, witnessing their experiments with disguise. Their small hands knock, their muffled voices call out threats and promises. I feign fear and amazement, and bestow handfuls of crackling cellophane. Each child who arrives at my door is a miracle. Each child is also the one who does not come and go from this house. I inhale their heady desire, map it against my own.

A young girl, maybe four years old, climbs up the steps. She carries a large plastic pumpkin, sings out her request. Her father, patient at the end of the walk, is enjoying himself in spite of the grim weather. I don't know this for certain, but it must be true. If I had this daughter, I would stand patiently at every walk in the city while she marched toward unknown doors.

I look at this tiny person, smudged whiskers on her cheeks. Unlike her peers, she has taken a few steps into the house before pausing. Her mission isn't as straightforward as the others' in this parade — she is investigating the world as she goes. She has an intrepid spirit.

I lean down to catch the full glory of her face. I offer her candy, she grins with appreciation. *What's your name?* I say. As soon as the words are out, I know I've been unwise. No child should be asked, not in a city. I am surprised at myself.

This girl checks out her pumpkin, the bodiless coats hanging on the hooks along the stairs. Then she looks back at me. *Chloe*, she says. She regards my living room casually.

I miss a beat altogether, fly heedless into a parallel universe, the one which accompanies all my dreaming hours.

Then I fly back, my heart thudding into place. *Of course you are*, I stutter. The little girl smiles at me, then turns and makes her way down the steps, through the looking glass, into a world distinct from mine.

NOVEMBER IS INTENSE. With university courses wrapping up in a month, wide-armed learning narrows down to pragmatic strategizing, and stress levels rise. I juggle the competing demands of classes and assignments and tests and essay consultations with waning stamina. And Chloe's birthday is hurtling toward me like a train. I am raw and vulnerable again. Even conversations with close friends are plagued with potholes.

In truth, I have no idea how to prepare for the birthday of a dead child, but I know I must. If I'm standing on the tracks when this train arrives, I will be flattened. I look at my calendar, I look at my teaching schedule, then I take my frayed nerves into the office of my department chair. *I don't know what to do, Ted,* I say. *I am already struggling to face my classes — I'm afraid it will be beyond me in that last week of November.* I wipe away tears with the palms of my hands, embarrassed by my fragility.

Ted leans forward, begins to lay out some options. Together we devise a plan to get me to December in one piece. I'll stay away from the university on Chloe's birthday, and again on her death day. In between I'll handle some classes and my colleagues will administer a few late-term tests. *I'll be here if you need help,* Ted says. *Just ask.*

My anxiety and sadness boil just below the surface for days, but when Chloe's birthday arrives, it's not what I have imagined. The hours have a thick, cloud-like hush about them, as if I've been drawn into a slower cycle of time — a gesture here might last a thousand years. Calm opens up inside me: I realize this is not a day to endure but a day to savour. I listen to music, I read, I replenish myself with sleep. As darkness begins eating away at the November light, I prepare a lavish meal and light dozens of small candles. When Bill arrives at the door, his arms are filled with flowers.

The evening draws down around us. In the soft light, we wander through the year, picking up precious moments, both jagged and smooth, and putting them in our pockets. We would never have imagined this path for ourselves, but it's ours. We have been changed by it, but we have not been destroyed. As the candles burn low, we celebrate the amazing fact of our daughter's life.

Winter 1997

FOR THE NEXT SEVERAL DAYS, we find ourselves being solicitous with one another, careful with ourselves, and cautious about the world. We need space and time to revisit our baby's life, and to look across the distance of a year at her death. We need space and time to revisit one another too — grieving is solitary, demanding work, and we have both been rewritten by it. On the anniversary of Chloe's death, we weep out our heartbreak, but we are together, and we are not afraid.

As December opens up, I realize that I have made it through my year of firsts. I will never again have to survive the first Christmas without Chloe, the first Mother's Day, her first birthday. Now I have precedence to cushion me, modest success to bolster my nerve. Gradually, I am able to catalogue other firsts as they float past: the first time I laugh without restraint, the first time I walk with vigour, the first time I hold a baby without flinching, the first time I say Chloe's name without weighing down the room.

Still, the terrain is rugged: many days, I am assaulted without warning by an avalanche of sadness. My outer self strives to meet the needs of my job and my home; my inner self pulls into a crouch, begging for relief.

I am demoralized by these bouts — they feel like weakness, lack of resolve. I have envisioned sorrow as an emotion that gets less intense and then dissipates entirely. I am discovering that it's more like a game of Snakes and Ladders — progress is neither predictable nor steady. At times I speed ahead, at others I stagger backward. It's hard for me to accept.

Late one January afternoon, I trudge down the stairs at the college. I am desperate for home, I need to escape the public zone. One of the administrators comes through the door after me, calls ahead to ask how I am. I look back over my shoulder, take in his expectant face — he's looking for the cheerful version of me, but I can find no trace of her. I pause at the landing, wait for him to catch up. *Not so good*, I hear myself say. *It's a hard, sad day.*

Concern and apprehension chase one another across his face. I understand: he's a reticent man, embarrassed by emotional display. I am about to scold myself when he reaches out and pats my arm. *It's such a difficult thing you're doing,* he says. We step into the outdoor wind, and head our separate ways. I feel less alone.

Spring 1997

WHENEVER I CAN STEAL A COUPLE OF HOURS, I disappear into my study to scout for words. I have a suite of crystalline winter poems, chilled with sadness. I have a handful of buoyant poems about the maternal body too. I begin tinkering with the nightmare transcripts — they're another voice entirely.

I look at the scatter of poems, and see my own self, cracked into pieces by Chloe's death. I am an archaeologist of sorts, retrieving fragments of a clay pot that sat too close to an ancient fire. I sift through the dirt, gathering pieces and fitting them together. I crouch for hours at the dig site, my back to the future.

While I painstakingly reassemble a past, a lot of life is going on in the present. I wear down Bill's reservations: I want to have another baby. Research is on my side. Subsequent pregnancies pose a much less serious risk of pre-eclampsia, and this time we would be monitored closely. No ambushes, not this round. Everyone would be on high alert. It's not that I'm immune to worry, but the baby call is a powerful one. So as winter gives way to spring, I begin another trek through the haze of morning sickness and fatigue. I feel wonderful.

Many days, I'm the only one who can make that claim. Our friends and families are jittery. They declare their enthusiasm, but their eyes betray them. They aren't certain they can step into the breach if we face another catastrophe. Bill orbits around me like a satellite, charting my blood pressure, indulging my peculiar cravings, encouraging me to rest. He does his best to manage his worry, but it's part of this journey for him. I learn later that he wept when my pregnancy was confirmed: he fears that this time he will lose me too.

It's not a difficult pregnancy, but it's not an easy one either — anxiety circulates around me like a fog. Still, I feel remarkably serene. I am a woman doing what women do. I have no illusions about what I risk. But I know something else, something delicate and wondrous. Life, even the smallest, shortest span of life, warms us all. As this new baby grows in me, I attend to it, I revel in it. If this child is destined for a life of days, I am determined to be present to every single one — even if they are days before breath, days in a maternal ocean. Above all, hope is a discipline.

Summer 1997

I FEEL STRONG AT HOME, but out in the world, I am vulnerable. As my belly swells, I bump into people who ask about the baby. There's something about pregnancy — it sweeps away reticence. *Is it your first?* they say. Mostly they are making conversation, sometimes they are genuinely interested.

I'm at a loss about how to respond. Answering *No* invites a follow-up, which inevitably leads to a head-on collision with suffocating sympathy or awkward dismay. I feel like a Venus flytrap, savaging unsuspecting passersby. Sometimes I choose to be more forthright: *No, I had a baby who died.* Still, it's challenging to receive a fact like that, and it takes courage to offer it too.

It's certainly easier to nod, smile, and move on, and often I do. But not answering truthfully also hurts me. I have a daughter who is already spectral. How dare I efface her further?

Gradually it dawns on me that I feel so compromised because I am carrying my own secret shame: I worry that I don't really know who this gone child is. I have so few shared moments to help me remember her, and the things I have — a few photos, a tiny hat, a handful of dates and numbers — feel more like obstructions than pathways. How can I find her? I am her mother. How can I not know?

I withdraw into my study and mull. I pull out all the poem sequences I've been working on and arrange them in front of me. This is where I must look, but I don't know quite what I am seeking. I peer a long time into the hall of words. I see anticipation and innocence. Mirroring back against them, I see terror and pain and desolation. Two halves of one story, starkly balanced, a fearful symmetry. The moments double and intensify, replicating as I watch. I steady myself. I understand that I'm looking at my own effort to tell my way back into wholeness.

Then I see that the crux of this story is missing: I have written no baby. Terror roars in my ears. I realize I have written no baby because I am afraid to call her, afraid she is beyond my call. I dread the silence, the absence, the lack of response. How will I recover myself from crushing silence? In the same instant I realize I have written no baby because I am afraid mere words will reduce her — and seduce me. How can I say what I cannot know?

I see what is required of me. In my writing and in my living, I must become a mother who is strong enough, brave enough, trusting enough to carry the mystery this infant girl embodies. I must birth my baby and allow her to die, and I must birth my baby and allow her to live. It's my task, and it's formidable.

I stand a long time at the edge of my anguish, and then I enter, tentatively. I'm following the traces of singers who sustain me in my pain — Betty Carter, Tom Waits, Nina Simone. It's not sweetness they traffic in, but something else, grit and heartache and rage and love. I imagine a lullaby with all those dimensions. I imagine myself at my child's side. I imagine her alive, I imagine her dead. I imagine her. This baby will not tighten her fingers around mine, she will not widen her eyes when she sees me, she will not relax her body against my heart. I will never collect her smiles. I will never bathe her or cut her hair. I will not spoon food into her mouth or help her shrug into a backpack for her first day of kindergarten. I will not see her grow.

Yet somewhere outside the dimensions of our bodies, I hold her. And in the quiet of my study, I sing to her. I hold her and sing to her in full knowledge that she is no longer living. I sing to her without a need for her to answer. I sing her a lullaby, a lament, a hallelujah. I sing her all that I know, and all that I don't yet know.

As my voice gathers strength, I take my place in the company of mothers whose love reaches their children in the dark as well as in the light, mothers whose love travels through trauma and leaps across devastation and even vaults over death. I am lifted and strengthened and heartened by this love. It is not something I choose, but something that chooses me. My love is my voice, my song, my path, my power. It pours through me, shapes my knowing. And as I lullaby Chloe, I understand that she is in my present as well as my past. She is my baby. I have a baby, and she is not gone from me. She is not gone.

Autumn 1997

WE MOVE THROUGH THE SUMMER AND INTO THE FALL. Bill has enrolled in the nursing program in London, an hour from Waterloo. His excitement about the clinical rotations easily balances out the frustration of commuting. I am scheduled to teach for six weeks — my enthusiasm for the classroom surprises me.

Every couple of weeks, we travel to Hamilton for an ultrasound and the specialist's stamp of approval. We inch up to the twenty-eight-week mark, the point at which Chloe arrived — then suddenly we're past it. By the end of September, five weeks shy of the due date, my pressure is elevated but only modestly. We are jubilant. We graduate into the care of our own obstetrician, and we begin to imagine having a baby at the Grand River Hospital just a few blocks from our home. A regular baby, a regular birth.

We sign up for the one-day prenatal class marathon. We didn't get a chance to do this preparation with Chloe, and though we know more than most new parents, our knowledge is skewed. We are determined to retrieve some innocence around this baby's arrival, invent a welcome that is open and celebratory.

On the first Saturday of October, twelve couples gather. We are directed to stake out our positions around the room's periphery and, at our leader's urging, introduce ourselves to one another. I can feel resistance blooming inside me. The nurse who's coaching us has far too much cheerleader in her for my taste, and the group is over-represented by twenty-year-old men with their ball caps on backward, joking about adjusting to less time for beer and motorcycles. By all indications, their partners have already adopted the long-suffering wife script. They grunt as they lower their bodies onto the mats and exchange knowing glances.

The hours stretch out. We see diagrams of maternal bodies and slides of fetuses at various stages of development. We watch an amusing cartoon about labour, then a few video clips. We practise supported breathing and try out various labour positions. The men count to twenty with a clothespin on their fingertip so they can experience the pain of contractions. The mood flips between embarrassment and excitement. I feel irritated. I don't want to be with these people — they have no idea what is ahead. They cannot imagine how fraught and precious and demanding it is. I fear for them.

We break for lunch, and the release is like a hit of oxygen. We head to a café across the street with a couple who are similarly out of place in this group. We talk cautiously, finding our footing. He's partway through a medical degree, she's a financial planner.

They are about to say more, then hesitate. *We lost a baby last year*, he says. *Still-born*. He reaches over and squeezes his wife's hand. *So this kind of day is really taxing for us.*

A heavy door swings open deep inside me. I don't have to lock up the safe with these people, I don't have to protect my precious, fragile treasure. Air rushes out of me, and questions, and concern. Bill and I cower at the thought of labouring to deliver a baby who is no longer alive. The other couple can't imagine watching a baby die. We tell our stories and entrust them to one another's keeping. Our babies find a place in this crowded café.

When we return, our instructor offers a whirlwind tour through the frightening back rooms of pregnancy: maternal illnesses of various sorts, and threats to infant health. This is her least favourite part of the day — that is clear. She gallops along, identifying warning signs and medical interventions, then downplaying the importance. *Don't worry*, she assures us, *only a handful of pregnant women experience this, less than two per cent are at risk for that...*

My jaw clenched as she launched into this topic, but after a couple of minutes, I am aghast. Has she forgotten that two of the couples here are among the walking wounded? We have sustained fear and agony more searing than anything she can imagine — and she would shrug off the danger? Surely it is her responsibility to honour the weight of what we're doing, to impress it upon these barely adult couples. Real birth is a long way from games with clothespins and panting patterns. Older than humans, birth is an occasion, like death, that catapults us into contact with forces that are at once terrifying and wondrous. None of us in this room is ever prepared for that. Not one. I seethe in silence. This flippant woman will not bring death into this room — and I'm too daunted to point out that death is always already present wherever people gather.

Neither our gone babies nor our heartbreaking trauma has any place here. I have felt this avoidance elsewhere, too, masquerading as courtesy, as if to skate past the blast site shows respect to those suffering. A new fierceness stirs in me: I can refuse to censor myself. My daughter lived, my daughter died. Her brief life is rewriting mine. To step around those facts prevents me from walking through the smoke and flames to bring back what I might learn.

Before we disperse to our various lives, our instructor gives us a tour of the hospital's labour and delivery wing. She ratchets up the excitement in her voice: each of us will come through these hallways in the next few weeks, and this place with its elaborate machinery and skilled staff will help us take home the prize of our dreams.

We walk the hallways, peer into rooms that stand at the ready. I am intensely curious. I can hardly imagine the forward drive of labour, let alone the transient population which will soon reach out to claim me. I'm also apprehensive, as if a woman with my history might somehow be tempting fate by prowling through places like these. It occurs to me that I am walking through this pregnancy with one foot in a magic world: I half-believe that spirit folk are in charge of this undertaking. It unnerves me to plan.

As we step into a delivery amphitheatre with its inscrutable machines and trays of shining instruments, our new friends veer away. I feel the sudden heart-drag in them both, and I know this is the place where their daughter was born. I take Bill's hand, and fall away from the instructor's chatter. I'm listening for the traces of a dead baby girl, and of all the other tender cataclysms and breathtaking miracles that float, sheer as hope, in this place. I listen. I can almost hear.

IT'S MID-OCTOBER WHEN I STEP INTO DR HALMO'S OFFICE. I'm not the woman who brought her unabashed excitement here nearly two years ago, nor the broken soul who came here after Chloe's death. Those earlier selves travel alongside me, I am stronger for their company.

I feel a certain fondness for this basement waiting room, the anonymous legs flickering past the window like bicycle spokes in the sunshine. I find a seat, adjust my posture, and try to ignore the urine sample, warm in my hand. I watch men perch beside their expansive wives, then relinquish these seats to the women who arrive every few minutes. It's unusually crowded — the doctor must have been delayed.

A very pregnant woman puffs in, hands supporting her heavy belly. I vacate my seat for her and lean against the wall by the oversized coats. Two women sit on the floor by my feet, a pregnant woman and her sister, maybe. They are poring over one of the many photo albums of babies delivered under this obstetrician's care. I have leafed through these assembled faces too, read the names, dates, weights, lengths. Despite their occasional shocks of orange or black or blond hair, babies look remarkably alike. They may be the best argument we have for citizenship in a single human family. The two women beside me flip from page to page, point, exclaim quietly to one another. This is her first baby, I think. You can feel it in her. I stretch and shift my weight.

One of the women stiffens. *Look*, she says to her friend. *Oh, this is terrible —*

I glance down and my eyes lock onto the small, floating footprints of Chloe's birth announcement. Death in the midst of all these births, a presence in this room of expectant women. A knell, the haunting none of us wishes to admit.

The woman and her sister chew their lips as they read. They can't imagine what they are looking at. They sit frozen for a long minute, then flip the page and wait for their distress to dissipate.

These two women have no idea that the mother of that dead baby is standing beside them, witnessing their alarm. I say nothing — what can be said? But I feel myself as a taint in this room. I was stricken by pregnancy. I bore a baby who died. I am the uninvited fairy at the debutante ball, the one who carries the dreaded curse. At the same instant, I realize that whoever assembles this ever-growing pile of photos came upon Chloe's pink parchment, and chose to include my baby among the other babies. A gratitude bigger than language sweeps up through me.

I regret the anxiety churning in the woman beside me — she is facing the blunt fact that none of us knows where the pregnancy journey is taking us. But I am satisfied for my lost child. She has a place in this flurry of faces. Her tiny feet walk here too.

BY LATE OCTOBER, I HAVE RELINQUISHED MY STUDENTS to the care of other professors. I lumber toward November 6, the date that has been circled on our calendar for months. My blood pressure is elevated but steady, and the baby kicks and turns. My parents arrive, and we whirl into action. Dad and Bill set up the crib. Mom and I sew receiving blankets and impossibly small sleepers. Small piles of softness, a welcome.

Against all expectations, I sail past my due date. Dad returns to Manitoba, and Mom takes to walking me briskly around the neighbourhood. The days crawl by, gather themselves into a week. Bill and I head to the hospital for a routine non-stress test. When we see the tape strip of the baby's heartbeat, a shudder of tears surges up and out of us both. I am, it seems, carrying a real baby, and the real baby is performing as it should in these cramped quarters. I remind myself to pack clothes and a toothbrush: apparently I will need them. The nurse, harried by her incessant pager, sends us home.

But now my breath catches on a new dread. What if this baby arrives on Chloe's birthday? I worry this problem like a guilty secret, finally blurt it out to my mom in a rush of tears. She considers it, then says simply, *You'll just put another candle on the cake each year. You'll celebrate them both.* We sit in the silence for a long minute. *It won't always be so painful,* she adds, and I can feel the weight of her own knowledge. In our family, we celebrated the birthday of a gone daughter just days before my birthday. I felt it as a privilege.

AT TWO WEEKS PAST THE DELIVERY DATE, I need to be induced. The hospital is overcrowded, so we have a few false starts before I'm finally hooked up to a drip. I'm glad of the tougher contractions, excited by their intensity. I breathe, I hold Bill's hand, I notice the bare white of this room, the meeting point of the mundane and the momentous.

In an hour, I am sucked under by the shuddering of a body at work. I'm mostly submerged, caught in the tides of this surreal world. I pull on Bill's hand to keep from drowning. When I surface, I gasp in air, blink away the blear, try to get my bearings.

The anaesthetist arrives. Apparently a labouring woman with high blood pressure is safer with an epidural. Nobody has bothered to explain this before, and I'm beyond arguing now. The nurse swings my legs over the edge of the bed, cautions me to hunch up my spine and stay still. Before the anesthetist can slip in the needle, I'm pulled away again into the body's shuddering. He waits, poised, works quickly when the contraction eases.

With the slow slide of numbness, the diving is less treacherous. I plunge under and subside, plunge under again. There's no time to breathe, but I'm not so anxious about that now. I am a pilot whale tumbled by the undertow. I'm watching for the arrival of the small swimmer. It will need protection in these devastating currents — it will need to be near its mother. I plunge deep, come up for air, plunge again. I am not myself.

Hours of diving, and I am only beginning to dilate. The doctor attaches a monitor to the baby's scalp, adding a pinging accompaniment to the groans of a maternal body. We settle into our work. Bill attends a woman who long ago left her intellect on the shore. The nurse approaches and retreats. The doctor and his apprentice appear and disappear.

When the monitor shrieks a warning, the nurse snaps to attention. She orders me to shift my body — the baby is in distress. I reposition myself, and the monitor returns to normal. We collapse again into our tasks, and I register nothing beyond the lack of my own breath, and the fact of labour, the literal, aching fact of labour. My body is striving toward a baby.

In twenty minutes, the monitor hikes into warning mode again. This time the flurry of activity around the bed has a different cast. *Call the doctor*, the delivery nurse barks. *The baby's heart has stopped again — call the doctor. We have to get that baby out of there.*

Whose voices? I can identify none of them, and yet they all belong to me. I need this baby. I need this baby not to die.

I'm whisked down the hallway, a body on a rolling bed. I am a scene, the site of a predicament. I refuse to say *catastrophe*. I refuse to imagine it. The doctors and nurses murmur as they wash, pull on sterile masks, gowns, gloves. Bill stands next to me, intense and focused. The anesthetist pumps his magical elixir into the epidural shunt, and my body numbs completely. The resident lifts his scalpel, prepares to lift a baby out of my abdomen.

I fear. I hope. I am beyond knowing.

When I hear the baby holler, something bursts open. *Oh!* I cry to the listening world. It's a sound, really, not a word. It's the sound of amazement rising up out of exhaustion and fear. It's the courage of breath — a mother's breath, a baby's breath. It's a new medium of attachment for us both. I tip my head toward the warming table, toward the circle of nurses and the weeping father. I cannot see this baby — this *boy* — but I am already tracking him, learning to follow his sound trail.

When they present him to me, a small white bundle, I see Chloe's face looking out from the folds of flannelette. I gaze at his round eyes, his full lips, the curve of his chin. Finally, I meet Bill's eyes. *He looks like Chloe,* I whisper. I settle back into my pillows. Bill closes his eyes and nods. He's as surprised as I am.

I can't hold onto any thought, not now. It is something after three in the morning, November 20, 1997. The baby snuggles in to nurse. I begin to drift. Bill stands next to us, our anchor.

TWO DAYS LATER, I AWAKE without the glaze of Demerol. It's a relief to be myself again, just clean post-surgery pain, uncomplicated by the confusion and nervousness connected with medication. I look around. I'm in a room on the ward, and the November sun is offering a thin promise of light.

The nurse appears on her silent shoes, carrying a swaddled soul who's begun to sing for his breakfast. I heave my incised self out of bed and into the chair, pile pillows on my lap. The nurse leaves, and this small wrinkled baby and I prepare for another attempt at nursing. I pick up the boy, my son, and hold him against my heart. He calms, and for a moment in the quiet of the morning, we're alone and at ease. The world waits on us.

Today is your sister's birthday, little dancer, I whisper to him, running my lips across his wispy hair. *Today is Chloe's day, and look, it's beginning to snow.* We gaze at the window, small eyes and large eyes, and it's true: the air is full of angels.

LIAM IS TWO WEEKS OLD WHEN I LAUNCH *lamentations*, the collection of mother-poems about Chloe. My colleagues, my students, my friends all gather on a grey Sunday afternoon — the room is packed. My mother is there, and Helen has driven up from Hamilton. Bill winds through the knots of people with our beautiful son, sleepy and small and absolutely safe in his father's arms. The atmosphere is celebratory. Even when the poems make us weep, we are happy. All of us are learning something new about what is lost and what is found.

By the middle of the December, I've pretty much recovered from the C-section, and Bill and I are finding our footing as new parents. Mom flies back home and we settle down to the business of being a family. On Christmas morning, we pass our precious baby between us, chatter over crumpled wrapping paper.

My sister has sent another angel: she kneels mischievously in the boughs of our Christmas tree, sprinkling stars.

1998

IN THE FIRST MONTHS OF LIAM'S LIFE, I discover how bewildering it is to care for a newborn. A baby disrupts your home, reorients your friendships, reconfigures your clock and your calendar. Like every new mother, I am both prepared and unprepared: this child and I are at one another's mercy, both of us learning as we go. I begin to master one skill when another demand presses in. Motherhood tests everything I know, and gives me answers I can barely interpret. It reveals my strengths, it exposes my limitations.

I realize I've been starving for exactly this textured experience of parenting. In the months after Chloe's death, I couldn't fathom what it meant to be her mother — the work of it was so abstract, so painful. With Liam, the beauty and chaos are literal, external to me. I can know the smell of his neck, and the way his weight settles against me. I can know his eyebrows, his fingernails, his ears, his old-man body. I can feel the slipperiness of his skin when I ease him into the sink. I can sense how time wraps around us in the dark hours of night when I rock and rock him.

I also discover how my shoulders ache when I've carried and soothed him, and how my breasts scream for weeks before we really work out the nursing challenge. I am desperately underslept, and have a hard time putting together a coherent trail of words, let alone a decent meal. Every person I encounter is a parenting expert eager to keep me from ruining this child. Every waking minute is intense, and when he falls asleep, I don't know whether to collapse or throw in a load of laundry.

Learning to be Liam's mother is exhausting, amazing, overwhelming, and inspiring. I discover what it means to be a precious face, a precious voice. I get to be a beginner, over and over. With this child, I have the luxury of time — we are building an edifice of all our gathered moments. My joy spills out like laughter.

AND SO WE ARE SWEPT INTO THE CHAOTIC WHIRL of our lives. I learn to know my son, I learn to know my maternal self. I become accomplished at heaving an awkward car seat into the back seat of our two-door sedan, I mind-read the differences between hunger and boredom and fatigue and discomfort, I master a million tricks to make this little boy giggle. Bill and I revel in his company, and find ourselves soaking up the present rather than focusing on the future or dwelling on the past. We learn to be our own particular family.

Chloe ghosts us, but softly. Because of her, I'm more aware of how vulnerable Liam is — how vulnerable I am too — but I am less apprehensive than I expected. It occurs to me I have learned something of my own strength, and of the strength in small bodies. Because of her, I am more mindful of the richness in every moment, more determined to pay attention. I am also aware that the present is a delicate thing, easily swamped. My task is to honour it with lightness, rather than with weight.

In a way, Chloe becomes a symbol for Bill and me, a reminder of our intention to live fully and thoughtfully. We strive, and in many ways we succeed. But we're hardly lifted above our own failings. Many days I chafe at my loss of freedom. I never get enough sleep, and many foods I love make my baby's stomach knot up in pain. I have too little time and energy to read, and nowhere near enough focus to write.

Months later, I return to the classroom and the pressure intensifies. One evening, Bill and I have a mean-spirited argument about which of us will bathe the baby — both of us are hemmed in by class preparation, neither of us has time. As the words cool in the air, I am chagrined: I would turn myself inside out for the chance to lay my hands on the body of my daughter, yet I rail against bathing my son. The lesson is so blunt, the choice so simple. I push my sleeves above my elbows, dig a clean pair of pyjamas out of the drawer, then scoop up the laughing boy. As I kneel beside the tub, I have to admit how much trouble I have staying fully present. I'm well-tuned to reach toward what is ahead and ache for what is behind, but to set those aside and attend to where I am? It requires a major re-orchestration of my own habits of mind.

Liam has no such challenge. Submerged in warm water and love, he has everything he can imagine. I run my soapy hands over his body and join him here in his delight.

The days knit themselves into months. Liam scrambles toward toddlerhood, a noisy, vibrant, joyful boy. He turns one in a hail of Cheerios. Two days later we light candles for Chloe, and fill the house with flowers. He is mesmerized by the petals shining in the soft light.

1999

THE NEXT YEAR IS A MAELSTROM. Seasoned parents laugh, then look wistful. *It doesn't last long,* they say, *so just enjoy it.* Some days I do enjoy it — the racket, the mess, the frenzied speed, the dash to stay one step ahead of this determined, whirling mass of energy. Other days it exhausts me beyond coping. How can every moment be so emotionally charged, so freighted with significance? The years may fly by, I think, but the minutes drag on and on and on.

Our circle of friends finally begins to relax around us. This parenting flurry is the life they've been dreaming for us; they're relieved that we have a chance to sink into it. I'm relieved too, and thankful — every single day I am. I know better than anyone that this is a wondrous story: I lost a baby, and I've been given another chance. I'm living out an old-fashioned fairy tale where good fortune redeems bad, and the kingdom returns to fullness.

Except that this story doesn't resonate for me. Now that I am many paces from Chloe's death and my own illness, I am less convinced that calamity is the most salient feature of that story. In fact, I am strong enough now to claim that it is actually my great fortune to be Chloe's mother. I have been entrusted with a task that is demanding, but also deepening. Mothering her is not something active, something literal. It's a long way from naps and cuddles and cubes of banana. It's a long way from keeping a vulnerable body safe, from celebrating new words, from supporting a child's growing awareness of others. Being Chloe's mother is something else entirely — not so much something I do as something I am. She leaves her elusive, delicate traces on the map of my self, and I am the one who is a child, learning to read this script.

I am full to bursting being a mother to Liam, but he didn't step into an empty place and make it full. He stepped into a full place, and made it fuller. I realize, as I stand in the midst of my toddler's clutter, that I am ready to set down my terror about forgetting my daughter and pick up the real challenge: to comprehend her. Chloe died but I didn't lose her. A child will always have a mother, a mother will always have her child.

2000

MY THIRTIES SLIP THROUGH THE HOURGLASS. Bill finishes his nursing training, finally hooking together his aptitude and his passion. I am pregnant once again, and this pregnancy is calm and healthy. I carry my fatigue and burgeoning belly through daytime classes, and when I curl up to rest, my rowdy toddler climbs in behind my knees with a posse of stuffed animals. By the time spring clears the sidewalks, Liam tears down the sidewalk on his tricycle, fierce with speed. I lumber after him, laughing at the cartoon spectacle we offer our neighbours.

On my thirty-ninth birthday in May, Bill is offered an academic posting in Winnipeg. We talk a long time before making a decision: I am loath to leave my colleagues and students and the security of work that fulfills me, but I would have more flexibility to mother these kids in their first years. I would have more freedom to write. And truthfully, I long for the prairie — the sky, the stretch of space. It is my heart's home.

Eight weeks later, we move. Beautiful Anna is three weeks old and Liam is halfway to three. For several months, our new house is in full renovation mode. Our lives are too. September arrives, and for the first year in many, I am not in a classroom. I am exhausted, busy, happy.

I am home.

2001-2005

THE FIRST FIVE YEARS OF A CHILD'S LIFE are the most physically intimate for a mother: I carry, cuddle, feed, rock, lift, grab, pat, bounce, restrain, swing, nudge, hug, stroke, clean, boost, sing to, and settle my children, often several times in the same day. And yet to hold them as they grow is like holding water in a fast-flowing stream: I can feel them in my hands, but it's motion that defines them. Their job is to grow, to strive toward their fullest, independent selves.

More than almost anything else, I see that Liam and Anna change. They change shape, they change size. Their skills change, their interests change, their ability to express themselves changes. They change their minds, they change their moods, they change their approach to the world. I hold them for a moment, and release them back into the stream of their lives. It is my pleasure, my privilege, even my obligation to stand on the bank and attend to them as they move.

I never feel as certain about how a parent attends to a child who dies. Other bereaved mothers speak of the age their children would be now, but Chloe exists in another dimension for me. Not exactly an infant, certainly not a child — it's like she has slipped out of time and moves free of the physical realm. If I find it challenging to hold two earth-bound changelings, it's many times more challenging to hold the daughter who floats free.

I think often, as I chase Liam and Anna through their childhood, that I'm undertaking two radically different kinds of mothering, but they show me the same thing: at the core of the task is something far closer to surrender than control. I am responsible for Liam and Anna, but it's clear to me that they exceed my grasp. My best option is to live with an open hand — at least I can cup the water for a few precious years.

Chloe? Released from the world I know, she exceeds me too. I wonder about my responsibility to her, about what settles in the palm of my hand.

WHEN ANNA IS NOT YET FOUR, she climbs into bed beside me, on the run from a nightmare. *There were two of you, Mama.* She hunches up to protect herself. *Exactly the same — same black and white hair, same face, same voice, same name. Two mamas.* She hesitates. *One of you,* she says, and her words choke in her throat. She swallows and tries again. *One of you said, "I don't need a daughter," and turned away from me.*

I can feel the horror spreading over my face. *Oh dear,* I mutter, *this is awful. What happened?*

I was so upset, she says. She tames her voice, determined to speak all of this. *I tried to grab ahold of you, Mama. I was crying, asking you to not leave. But you just said, "I don't need a daughter," and you turned and began to walk away. Oh Mama, it was so sad — I was so sad!*

I put my arms around her, nestle her up against me. *I wouldn't leave you, honey,* I whisper, soothing her back toward sleep. *I would never walk away from you. I will always need a daughter — you're a precious part of my life.*

She drifts to sleep and I lie in the quiet for a long time, thinking about the doubled mother. Anna is right. One of me stays within reach of my children — the maternal self who's invented and restored, endlessly, by the attention of these two young beings. My other self is always turning to walk away from them, into a life that's inconceivable to this child or her brother, a life built of the intersections with others, with words, with dreams, with sorrow and hope and boredom and determination, confusion, ache, desire.

And there are many kinds of turning away in Anna's world. I have started a new job — one that allows me to work with writers and readers in my city. The learning curve is steep, and the work is intense. Anna can feel the way it redirects my attention and energy.

What's more, Bill and I are no longer able to travel so well in tandem. Many nights we settle our children for sleep then talk late, sorting out differences and exploring ways to conceive of a family that doesn't all live together under one roof. No matter how cautious and considerate we are, both Anna and Liam are frightened by these shifts — it's not easy for them to be changing so dramatically when the groundwork of their lives won't hold still.

Anna feels the twinning in her dream as a searing loss, but she is a twinned character too, as is her brother. They are also the ones who turn away from me, head out into a world where I may not follow. Every day they make their forays, every day they gain more ballast. I watch them, in wonder. Part of me sends them out and calls them back. Part of me turns away into my own life.

I am like Anna, a rooted being — leave-takings have torn me open since I was young. I realize, as I listen to Anna sleeping beside me, that I missed the chance to learn how to let Chloe step free of me. Her death consolidated years of abstract dread in me, channeled them earthward in a blast that threatened to burn up everything. But I see now that living in two worlds is partly a gift we offer the people we love: we thrive when someone we trust holds us, and we thrive when we can explore our independence.

My dreaming daughter and I are connected, deeply and powerfully, and we are also separate, independent. The same is true of my ethereal daughter.

Mom? It's Liam's voice, and this is the conversation we specialize in: me driving somewhere while my back-seat philosopher ponders the universe. *Mom, did you know you have to hold your breath when you go past a graveyard? It's so the spirits won't get into your body.*

We drive awhile in silence. I'm working on this little piece of information, wondering when I stopped feeling anxious about graveyards. As kids, my sister and I walked some Sunday afternoons up to the small cemetery in Boissevain. I remember the turnstile, the gravel path winding forward into the quiet. We'd cut sideways through the older stones, making exaggerated detours to avoid stepping on the dead, until we reached the wide road up the middle. Then we'd head east, watching for the headstone that marked my sister's grave. White marble and mystery, a point of access to a baby I'd never seen.

I don't remember being anxious then, only aware of a certain timbre to the place, a hush like fallen feathers. But my son knows it's dangerous — the spirits can get inside your skin.

So, Liam says over the car's hum, *you have to hold your breath, Mom. If you're superstitious*, he adds. *Which I am.*

I guess I'm not particularly superstitious, I say. *And I suppose I know a few people whose spirits I wouldn't mind having inside my skin.* Now that's a dangerous opening — I realize it as soon as the words are out.

Chloe, he says from the back seat. *You mean Chloe, right?*

Well, yes, Chloe, but also some other special people in my life who are now dead. I begin the catalogue in my head. I think, without intending to, about the people who will be added. Many will be sooner than I would wish.

After a minute, he asks, *Where did you bury Chloe?* I realize we've never talked about this part of her story.

We didn't bury her, love. When people die, you can choose to bury them, or to have their bodies turned into ash. So no, we didn't bury Chloe.

Liam is snagged in the middle of this. *Turned to ash?* he says, and I can hear the implications yawning open beneath him. It's a big topic. I'm not sure I have the nerve for it just now, not in a car buffeted by city traffic. I aim to settle him with the simplest sketch: once a body is no longer alive, it doesn't stay the same. All bodies return to earth finally.

We travel quietly for a few blocks.

You should have buried Chloe, he says finally. *Then we could go and visit her. That would be good.*

I think of the white marble stone in my childhood. It *was* good.

We lived in a different city, sweetheart, so that would have made it harder for us now, don't you think?

In the silence, I can hear his seven-year-old mind working through the logistics of being alive, being dead.

But still, he says. Now his voice has an edge. *Still, Mom, I can't believe you burned up your daughter.*

Without warning, I'm that earlier self, watching a box of ash come home, an unremarkable shoebox, container for a life. All these years later, the complicated pain of it settles lightly in my lap. I appreciate Liam's bluntness. It's the only way to speak this piece. And he's right too: there is no answer for it. Except that even an act of such blazing finality can be an expression of love.

There are many ways to respect the dead, I say to my son, curious and brave in the back seat. *Burning is one way, burying is another.*

Breathing deeply as I drive by graveyards might be one to adopt, I think to myself. Inviting the spirits in.

To my surprise, Chloe's presence in our family becomes more and more definite as the years tumble past. Even when he has moved into a new home, Bill sends flowers every year on her birthday, and we fill our houses with candlelight. The kids and I plant an amaryllis together a week later and watch it burst into glorious blooms as the new year begins. Every Christmas, we unpack the ever-expanding assortment of angels my sister seeks out for me and hang them on our tree.

Mostly we talk. Liam and Anna are full of ideas about where she is, what she knows, what it means to be dead. Sometimes they feel troubled — death is hard for any of us to understand. More often they are curious, open, tender. They have a sister.

When Anna is about five, she sits a long time at the table, working on a drawing. Finally, she calls me over to look at it. A beautiful princess stands in the middle of the page. She is wearing a glorious gown, but she is weeping — the tears run down her cheek in a line. A rainbow arches tight around her. It's almost as if she stands in a doorway of colour. Her hands hang at her sides. Off to the left, afloat in the whiteness, is a small oval. I look carefully to understand what it is. An oval with a smaller circle toward one end, and yes, a face in the circle: dots for eyes, a curving smile. A swaddled baby.

I sit next to my daughter, who watches me look at her drawing. *Tell me*, I say.

Well, she says, *this is Chloe.* With a majestic sweep, she indicates the princess.

And she is very sad? I ask.

Yes, says Anna. *She is very sad because she cannot play with me.*

So this is you? I gesture toward the little oval. She nods, and her artist's satisfaction flies loose in the room. She climbs off the chair and heads into her life.

I look at the little baby she's drawn, all wrapped up. The baby smiles: she feels loved, she feels safe. The beautiful princess stands in her dazzling portal and weeps for what she has missed. These sisters are separate. These sisters are connected.

I think a long time about this vision Anna has offered me. Both my children have an ease that I don't know. They are sad about Chloe, but they are confident about loving her — it doesn't occur to them that they might not know how to go about it. She just is, and they just do.

2006 - present

IT STUNS ME WHEN I CAN SAY TEN YEARS HAVE PASSED since Chloe was born. Ten years — it sounds so substantial, so solid. I take stock. I am more settled than I was in the first years, that's clear. I am healthy again. I am busy at a job I love, and filled with wonder over my growing kids. Many things have changed in my life, some of them dramatically, but I have flex in my knees. I feel myself becoming more tuned-in, more responsive, more creative. I am, I realize, deeply and soulfully happy.

That's not to say I'm immune to patches of aching sadness. My heart snags readily on stories and images and snatches of melody. I am attuned to sorrow in ways that I could not have imagined before. But it no longer frightens me, and it fills me rather than empties me.

Each year, I carve out solitude around Chloe's birthday. In the early years, I was defending myself against the assault of a world that was too literal, too noisy and insensitive. I needed to hide. As my sorrow becomes less jagged, I find I am anticipating November rather than dreading it. I feel it as a special time, creative and peaceful. I read. I write. I think. I dream. I set aside the racket and celebrate my daughter's life and my own learning. I protect that time not because I am afraid of it but because it is precious to me.

As my fear wanes, I am able to speak about Chloe more freely. I'm prepared for people to shy away from the subject, but I have courage enough to hold us aloft until we find our way through.

And I am surprised, over and over, by the number of people who want to share their own lost babies — babies they have carried or miscarried, or babies who figure in their families or the families of their friends. I talk with people who are missing siblings, people whose pregnancies have failed, people who are unable to soften the sorrow of grieving friends. So much silence around these infant wraiths, and so much tenderness too. Some of the stories are current. Others have been waiting for decades, occasionally even generations — yet the years amount to nothing. Thirty-two years or eight months, it hardly matters: there is something so searing about that moment when a dreamed future turns away from you that time cannot smooth it out. The time around scars, painful and precious.

I struggle always to find the language. For years, I've been uneasy with euphemistic habits that allow people to pass away rather than die, but to say *I have a dead baby* feels coarse, like filthy hands at a meal. Often I say, *I had a baby who died*, though that locks her into the past, which doesn't feel accurate either. Sometimes I say, *I lost a child*, but that leaves me feeling forlorn and irresponsible. I begin to say, *I have a gone baby* — it's a little awkward, but at least it gives us both some agency.

One day, a friend of mine settles back in his chair, then says, *I don't understand why you speak of Chloe as gone.* The comment stuns me. *Because she is*, I want to say, but that answer sounds suspect, even to me. I carry around the comment for weeks, like a grain of sand inside my shell.

I begin to practise: *I have two daughters*. It occurs to me that my aunt continues to be right. Some gifts are hard to receive.

I HAVE ANOTHER FAVOURITE from amongst Anna's drawings. This one appeared on my fridge one day when Anna was about seven. The girl is stretched diagonally across the page. She offers us her profile — a pert nose, one eye with perfect lashes, well-defined lips. Her body is less detailed, though you can see her toes. She is held aloft by spectacular wings. Several clouds float on the white of the page.

WOW! says the angel. Her pronouncement threatens to burst her speech balloon.

I love this angel. She has vitality, she has nerve, she has feeling — just like the artist who caught her in this moment of flight and amazement. Even better, this buoyant creature is not alone. Another pair of feet, small and distant, hovers at the top of the page, so presumably there are others outside the frame. For Anna, the sky really is full of angels.

I keep the drawing on my fridge for months and months. The angels make me laugh every time I pass them. *Wow!* they say, zooming around in ethereal wonder. They're checking us out, I figure. They're thrilled that we have a chance to experience our earthly trek. They remember the taste of strawberries, the late light of a July evening, the way a lullaby purrs in the throat of a singer and the ear of a beloved. They remember fatigue and anger and fear and pain. They remember comfort and surprise and joy. They remember sorrow, they remember hope, they remember love. They say *Wow!* to the whole messy tangle of it, because it's all amazing.

I pull this picture out of my treasure drawer a couple of years later, just after my dad's death. A strange brew of feelings is roiling around inside me — terrible sadness, also peacefulness, and something else entirely, something like euphoria. *I'm eighty,* he said, when he told his kids about his diagnosis. *This is not a tragedy — this is life!* Then he proceeded to golf and fix things around the house and enjoy the parties thrown in his honour.

My father and I talked often about death. He told me it was more shattering to watch his baby girl die than to contemplate his own death. I understand that, too. I mourn him deeply, but I feel no anguish. I have learned something elemental in my experience of Chloe—something about releasing someone, about trusting the vitality of love to continue to animate you when that person has turned away.

He soaked up the world and his treasured people in full consciousness of his mortality. From June until November, he warmed the people around him, talking and listening. He teased us and he held us. He paid attention. As his body lost its strength, he became lighter somehow, as if he were gradually stepping free of a garment he'd worn lovingly for eight decades. His life came to a graceful cadence, in contrast to his daughter who struggled with pain for most of a year, or Chloe who moved through her short life with terrible urgency, or the little being I miscarried before her who had an even briefer and more mysterious encounter with this world.

But my father is right: this is life. We are living, we are dying. We cannot know anything more certain, and we cannot know anything more mysterious. I look at Anna's angel, exclaiming her wonder, and I see my father, arms thrown around his own life with such appetite and such respect. I look around me, and tune into the wow of it all.

CHLOE'S SPECIAL, LIAM SAYS. He's older now, half past twelve. He's in the front seat now, and I feel him like a counterbalance, strong and definite at the edge of adolescence.

The observation floats there, like the imprint of a camera flash. We haven't particularly been speaking about Chloe, though I'm in the final throes of this book, so she's not far away. *Tell me what you know of her,* I say. *Tell me what you mean.*

We drive in silence for a bit while he figures out where to start. *Well, of course I never met her,* he says, *but I kind of have a sense of her. She has a certain feeling for me—playful, like a child.*

So does she seem like a child to you? I ask. *Or a baby?*

She's not like a child, Mom. She's like, hm, she's like — He stutters to a halt, and then laughs. *Well, you can't really capture it in words, I guess. She gives me a feeling, that's as close as I can say it. Like when I think I know how things are clicking together and then there's a completely different outcome — I have the sense of her then. It's sort of like a little giggle, like she's enjoying the fact that I've been surprised, like she's teasing me about it.*

I look across at this boy. There's been more than enough death around him recently. His father's closest friend died a few days ago after a long illness. His beloved grandfather died with all of us around him just before Christmas. Our little household has been taxed by the sorrow and loneliness, and obviously it's not just me who's been pondering the what-is-it of death, the incomprehensible mystery that ghosts us all.

I kind of get a different sense about different people who've died, Liam offers. *Like with Grandpa, I have more of a let's-figure-out-how-this-works feeling. With Chloe, it's more like teasing. It's hard to explain, but it makes me feel stronger. I'm less afraid now of all the stuff I feel but can't touch.*

I scan the expanding list of people I mourn. I think of my wise and funny father, and my beloved aunts. I think of treasured friends, so much closer to my own age, some of whom have died, some of whom have sidestepped death but live with a more pressing sense of the clock. I think of people I have loved and have lost to the fault lines of changing lives. I feel them, particular and specific. I feel them because they have shared something real with me — and I have received them, however imperfectly. If they have affected me, I carry their imprint. I carry them forward.

I love that my son feels his sister as a little sprite. It seems a feat of imagination or perception to take the print of a personality in the absence of proof — it's that dearth of information that has knocked the air of out of my lungs so often over the past decade and a half. *But who is she?* I have asked myself. *How can I know her if there are no stories?*

I ride along next to this remarkable boy, and it strikes me that I knew him from the first moment. There was something particular and identifiable in him when he was born, and I feel it in him still, a force that moves him and moves through him. I know him better now because I have a huge cache of stories, but I wasn't wrong in the first place.

It occurs to me that I can set down my outrage about having such limited experience of my Chloe. I *felt* her — we felt one another. Even clouded by illness, she was fierce and determined, a little spitfire. Why doubt now what I knew then?

We pull into the garage. *Thank you, Liam,* I say. He smiles. Then he leans over and gives me a kiss.

ANOTHER HOT DAY. I hang clothes on the clothesline, listen to the inexhaustible song scrolling in my head. *Summertime, and the living is easy.* I've been accompanied by songs as long as I can remember, but it's only in the last few years that I've started to hear them like subtitles thrown up by my subconscious. I shake out a kid's T-shirt that's nearly as big as my own and swipe at a mosquito settling on my arm. The mosquitoes are prodigious this year, so the living is not exactly easy — we're all busy doing the slap dance.

Fifteen years ago I lived in another house in another city. At the edge of that summer, I padded through my house in the loosest clothes I could find, alert for any spot that would afford me five minutes of sleep. Couch, floor, chair. Sometimes I would press my cheek into the cool tabletop and rest. Once I dozed off leaning against a door jamb. These were the earliest weeks of Chloe's presence in my life, a marathon of fatigue and nausea, diffuse and perpetual effort.

I don't remember "Summertime" humming in my inner ear in those torpid days, but it was the song that rose up unbidden when I stood in the glare of the NICU and reached for my daughter's tiny fingers. *Summertime*, I sang, softly, softly, *and the living is easy.* I was sharply aware of the swirling ironies. Outside the hospital, November was taking a machete to the last leaves. Inside this room, Bill was propped against a wall of exhaustion, I was patched together and barely standing, and Chloe, potent little being, was forging a path between bigger seasons. The living was not easy, not for any of us.

I was aware of the ironies but I wasn't seeking them out. I was only thinking about placing my mother-self into the ear of my daughter, about buoying her up, even slightly, with the love curled up in a lullaby. As my voice slipped past the lump in my throat, it dawned on me that this song was committing me to speak a truth to myself and to my child. *One of these mornings,* I murmured, *you're gonna rise up singing. Then you'll spread your wings* — screech of pain, future smashing into present — *and you'll take to the sky.* Dread, alarm, choke of tears. But the thread of a song is strong, and can wind its way through fear. *Until that morning there's a-nothing can harm you* — is it possible? — *with Daddy and Mama standing by...*

Daddy and Mama. I look across years and see us standing by. We couldn't protect our baby from harm. We couldn't protect ourselves either. We watched that tsunami roll toward us, and we braced ourselves for the impact. Neither of us could conceive of it, and even after all these years, it drenches me. Bewilderment, sadness. And now, having become acquainted with my grief, something strong and durable. I might call it wonder, or love.

The dragonflies dart and hover near my clothesline. Clearly, they're more inspired by the mosquito population than I am. I stand quiet a moment, listening to the dry click of their wings. I love dragonflies — these burly black ones, the electric blue ones with their needle-slender bodies, the deep burgundy one that landed on my shoulder a few summers back and looked at me with its 30,000 eyes. Bill and Liam gave me a dragonfly pendant when I was pregnant with Anna, and I realize I have come to associate these creatures with motherhood. I suppose it's their ungainly grace and occasional ferocity — plus the expectation that they'll accomplish pretty much everything while in full flight.

When I was eighteen, I witnessed the emergence of dragonflies. The nymphs are wingless things, all lumpish body and spindly legs. They crawl out of marshes and up grass stems, then cling there, waving in the spring breeze. I was hiking with a friend who spotted them. If I'd been on my own, I would have tramped through a miracle and missed it.

We crouched down and the patch of grass was alive with nymphs, thirty or more, each on its own stem, waiting. Then, as I watched, their backs split open — it hardly seems possible until you're looking at it. Their backs split open and their wings, hidden all this time in bunched-up packets, begin to open out into the air. The rest of the body wriggles out of the exoskeleton and grips the stem until the wings are rigid and ready for flight. It's painstakingly slow, this process, slow and deliberate. After an hour or more passed, my friend and I were surrounded by new dragonflies, flexing their wings in the late May sunshine. Then on some invisible cue, they rose up, airborne for the first time, and flew into their adult lives.

My friend and I rose up too, and stood watching the new flyers. When we finally turned away, I realized the ground around us was littered with abandoned bodies, eerily translucent and perfectly intact, apart from their split backs. I picked my way through, unnerved by the emptied husks, and shuddering at the inevitable crunch under my feet. *These creatures aren't dead*, I kept reminding myself, and I knew that was true — but I had no name for what remained in the grass.

How to love an absent being, perhaps that's the troubling question that crouches at the heart of grieving. In the weeks after Chloe's death, it was both an untenable proposition and an obsessive need: a precious dream had been stolen, and my stunned self hovered in dismay, tireless searcher. Only a shell attended to the world which whispered against my body. At that stage, loss is torture, a heart carved from a living body. It's desperation and the clench of phantom pain — love as anguish.

It's true that being Chloe's mother has taxed me. I have been frightened and dazed and grim. I have nearly drowned myself in tears. And that emotional turmoil is justified — it might be the biggest work of our lives, making room for others in the sanctum of our selves, then releasing them when they must fly. But as the intensity of the disturbance subsides, I see the question still, like a stone at the bottom of a still pool. How do you love an absent being?

I look a long time, and see that the answer is there too. After days, weeks, months, years of aching for her, it dawns on me that I will never be without this dream-daughter who is something more and something less than imaginary. She is not someone I remember, but someone I know. She may not be alive, but neither is she absent. And love? It is not something I do, not something I bestow. It's bigger than I can comprehend, and unpredictable, like weather. Love is my elemental connection with Chloe — it is a medium we share, a force that makes sense of us both. I understand it no better than I understand death, but I know I am in it, absolutely and irrevocably. It connects me to others, to the earth, to thoughts, to beauty. It blesses me and challenges me. It is air for my spirit.

I finish hanging up damp clothes amidst the backyard aerobatics of the dragonflies. Within sight of a half-century, I am in my summertime. Sometimes the living is easy, yes, and sometimes it is not. A good life needs tribulation the way a good story needs controversy—remove it and you can miss the point. Devastation and revelation, the Janus faces of awe.

Death is a force to be reckoned with, and I suspect none of us are fully prepared for its shock waves. It's not so much an event as an encounter with the unthinkable that shakes us at the core of where we live. I consider my scarred self, my arduous trek, the brilliant blessing of days opening up, one after another. Some descents offer you better vision, stronger lungs, more nerve. Wreckage can bless you, I believe that now. Wreckage can crack you open, make more space for the world to get in. Love is my dance partner in this waltz of pain and celebration, and here I am again: out of grief, singing.

Acknowledgements

Segments of an earlier version of this book appeared in *Prairie Fire* (winter 2004). I thank the editorial board for their encouragement, and for nominating my work for the Western Magazine Awards. I am grateful to the Canada Council for the Arts and the Manitoba Arts Council, whose support allowed me to get this project well begun, and to Karen Haughian at Signature Editions who coaxed it out of hiding, and then guided me with intelligence and generosity toward its completion.

I have been enriched by the people who appear in these pages; I thank each of you for sharing the rocky path with me. For helping me find my way through the writing of this story, I offer special thanks to Gary, Janet, Tannis, Susan, Steve, Phyllis, Heather, and Bill. For keeping me balanced en route, I'm grateful to my wonderful THIN AIR team, the *dig! magazine* crew, and the writers and jazz musicians whose creativity we celebrate.

My whole life is a joyful song to my mom, Anna Grace, and my dad, Les; I'm only beginning to understand what a privilege it is to have been well-parented. I reserve my deepest thanks for my children, Liam and Anna, for their brilliant company and boundless love.

The Author

Charlene Diehl is a writer, editor, performer, and the director of THIN AIR, the Winnipeg International Writers Festival. She did her graduate work at the University of Manitoba, receiving a PhD in 1992 under the supervision of Robert Kroetsch. After a post-doc at McGill, and seven years as a professor in the English Department at the University of Waterloo, she returned to Winnipeg in 2000. She has published essays, poetry, non-fiction, reviews, and interviews in journals across Canada, and has to her credit a scholarly book on Fred Wah as well as a collection of poetry, *lamentations*, and two chapbooks, *m^m* and *The Lover's Handbook*. Excerpts from *Out of Grief, Singing*, which appeared in *Prairie Fire*, won a Western Magazine Gold Award. She was the featured poet in the fall 2007 issue of *CV2*. When she's not chasing literary language (or her two speedy pre-teens), she edits *dig! magazine*, Winnipeg's bi-monthly jazz publication.

Eco-Audit
Printing this book using Rolland Enviro 100 Book
instead of virgin fibres paper saved the following resources:

Trees	Solid Waste	Water	Air Emissions
4	127 kg	11,982 L	278 kg